I0887074

Pulling Back the Curtain

ON THE FORMER SOVIET UNION

R. FRANKLIN COOK AND CARLA D. SUNBERG

THE FOUNDRY
PUBLISHING®

The Foundry Publishing®
PO Box 419527
Kansas City, MO 64141
thefoundrypublishing.com

ISBN 978-0-8341-4379-1

Printed in the
United States of America

Cover design: Caines Design
Interior design: Sharon Page

Library of Congress Cataloging-in-Publication Data
A complete catalog record for this book is available from the Library of Congress.

10 9 8 7 6 5 4 3 2 1

Dedication

This book is dedicated to all the people who are not mentioned in these pages, for they are too many. All of those who came and served, missionaries and volunteers alike. All of those who helped us in those early days, all across the former Soviet Union. It was a great cloud of witnesses. And to all those who became a part of the community of Nazarenes. Thank you!

Contents

Foreword

GROWING UP IN SCOTLAND in the 1960s and 1970s, even as a young boy, I was well aware of the reality of the Cold War that had developed after World War II between the United States, the United Kingdom, and the Soviet Union with their respective allies.

The metaphor of an "iron curtain," first used in this context by former British prime minister Winston Churchill in a speech in 1946, really did describe well the political, social, military, ideological, *and spiritual* barrier that was erected by the Soviet Union to separate itself and its dependent allies from contact with and influence from the West and non-Communist countries.

This separation and its impact globally were real. History now tells us of the suffering behind this curtain and the misconceptions this separation caused on both sides, with the inherent and genuine dangers to the whole world. On both sides of the curtain, we all knew who our enemy was and what threats they represented.

Yet in all this time, as in every time and in all circumstances, God was at work. We know he loves all people, in every country and in every situation, so he was at work, in ways perhaps inconceivable and unrecognizable. As Nazarenes who believe passionately in his prevenient grace, God was at work on both sides of the curtain. And as we know from the life, death, and resurrection of Jesus, God has previous experience in tearing down curtains that divide, from top to bottom.

In due course, in the 1980s and 1990s, the Iron Curtain was pulled back, the previously unbreakable walls were broken down, and the gaps that appeared left openings in every way, giving the church opportunities that previously did not exist.

The wonderful story shared so powerfully by Dr. Cook and Dr. Sunberg in *Pulling Back the Curtain in the Former Soviet Union* details what God was doing and what he did in establishing the Church of the Nazarene in the former Soviet Union. It is a story of miracles, grace, salvation, and transformation.

As former regional director of the Eurasia Region, I had the privilege of building on the legacy of Dr. Cook and others who succeeded him in this role and then working with Drs. Carla and Chuck Sunberg when Carla was our jurisdictional general superintendent. These humble spiritual giants had all been key figures in the story of God's work through the Church of the Nazarene to establish and develop the mission there, and I am so grateful to them for their vision, passion, compassion, and courage in taking the first steps in this new era for the church in that significant part of Eastern Europe.

Now in my role as global missions director I am so thrilled to read their stories, celebrate God's faithfulness, and be reinvigorated in our calling to make Christlike disciples in the nations, to the ends of the earth, knowing that we serve a God for whom nothing is impossible. I commend this book wholeheartedly to all who are passionate about missions.

—Jim Ritchie
Global Missions Director

Prologue

FRANKLIN

TO OUR READERS OF A CERTAIN AGE, there are words from the Cold War (1947-91) that will have a ring of familiarity and a chill of foreboding. To younger readers, some of these same words will have little or no meaning. Or, at best, they will be terms from a history book or class. Here are a few: "ABM" (antiballistic missile), "arms race," "brinkmanship," "Checkpoint Charlie," "containment," "détente," "first-strike capability," "Iron Curtain," "mutually assured destruction," "perestroika," "summits," "SALT" (Strategic Arms Limitation Talks), "glasnost," "Soviet."

It is not our purpose to define or describe these and many other terms in the lexicon of a historical period, but to point out that in this book we are talking about an atmosphere in which the prospect of "mutually assured destruction" was a dark reality that haunted the minds of most people. The Soviet Union had morphed following World War II into a military adversary of the United States and the Western World. It was a bleak time, one in which the Iron Curtain had forbidden travel and communication. Radio signals were blocked, television images banned, and reporters highly restricted. Almost every world event of this era was bifurcated into two parts. There were the "good guys" and the "bad guys." There was mistrust and misunderstanding. The spy industry flourished as the KGB ([Soviet] State Security Committee) and the CIA (Central Intelligence Agency) tried to outmaneuver each other.

The Soviet Union was often described as a "transcontinental" federal union of fifteen national republics, with the largest being Russia. It spanned much of Eurasia, covering eleven time zones, including parts of Europe and Asia. Following the 1917 Russian Revolution, it was the de facto successor to the Russian Empire of the czar regime. It was governed by the Communist Party and was a self-proclaimed secular state. Karl Marx, the philosophical "father" of Communist doctrine, had proclaimed organized religion to be the "opiate of the people," and thus the new Soviet government tried by every means possible to stamp out religion, religious belief, or religious practice. They closed all monasteries except for four, executed thousands of priests and pastors, and created a spiritual vacuum that could be filled with the Soviet dialectic. The Soviet government gave high priority to education, increasing literacy from 28 percent at the time of the Revolution to nearly 100 percent by 1991. Women were given the right to vote universally early on (the nobility had been given the right to vote in the mid-nineteenth century). The government tried to reshape human character and life into the ideal "Soviet Man or Woman" (*Homo Sovieticus*) whose primary motive was for the "collective good." The economic system was a "command economy," and as a result, the value structure was in great contrast to that of the West.

It is important to remember that at the time of the Revolution in 1917, the Church of the Nazarene as a merged denomination was only nine years of age. It was in the early days of its existence, feeling its way, knowing its beliefs, but dealing with a great variety of practices regionally around the United States and, to a lesser extent, in Canada and the United Kingdom.

There was a strong mission impulse accompanying the various merging groups, having brought forward sponsored work in India, the Cape Verde Islands, Guatemala, and several other places. The DNA of missions along with the global burden for evangelism was already planted in the new denomination and heavily promoted by General Superintendent Hiram F. Reynolds. This global stamp on the church not only survived but also has thrived to this day.

The reality facing the Church of the Nazarene between 1989 and 1993 was what to do in a changed world. The breach of the Berlin Wall and the subsequent opening of the Iron Curtain, the end of the Cold War, and the dissolution of the Soviet Union changed everything. Suddenly people could travel, news was allowed, and treaties were signed attempting to limit the "arms race." What would, what could, what should the Church of the Nazarene do? There was no plan in place, no strategic document to guide, no financial resources held in reserve for this new contingency—this new open door.

What is more important, there was no experience, no history, no legacy. That part of the world had been religiously Orthodox, adhering to the traditions of the Eastern Church. We of the West did not know the language, the customs, or the protocols. Facing us was this huge new opportunity, perhaps the greatest and most complex ever confronting the Church of the Nazarene. Would the church ignore, shirk, or confront?

What you will read in this book is a small sampling of what followed and what resulted, of how resources were found, people were engaged, and the foundation was laid. Against almost impossible odds, amazing miracles began to emerge from the void. Looking back, those of us who were directly involved find it hard to explain rationally—in fact, it can only be explained (or not explained, if you prefer) spiritually.

Introduction

CARLA

No, not under a foreign heavenly-cope, and
Not canopied by foreign wings—
I was with my people in those hours,
There where, unhappily, my people were.
—Akhmatova, *Requiem*

LARISSA WAS A HAPPY LITTLE GIRL, enjoying life in downtown Moscow with her mother, father, and younger sister. The party was providing for all their needs, since her father faithfully served the new leader of the nation, Joseph Stalin. Trained as an attorney, he was part of the inner circle, providing guidance and a listening ear to those impassioned by the ideology of Marxism. The reward for his loyalty was the promise of an apartment in a building being constructed along the Moscow River, within view of the Kremlin. While the family was waiting for the completion of that project, they lived in a communal apartment, with the four of them living in one room, all the while sharing the kitchen and bathroom with two other families. This did not bother them, because they were willing to sacrifice everything for the motherland.

Days were filled with attending school and learning what it meant to be a young Communist, or Pioneer. Loyalty to the cause was of utmost importance because the Soviet Union would surely be an instrument of peace for the entire world. Children earned pins and badges that reflected their willingness to support the party. Summers were filled with Pioneer camps and hours working the land and embracing Communism. Larissa's mother was a doctor, serving for meager pay, but joyfully, because she knew that her work was for the utopian vision. One day, Communism would spread everywhere in the world, and there would be no more pain or suffering.

One dark day, all the dreams came crashing down. Larissa's beloved father was home with the family when the KGB officers arrived. Almost immediately, they grabbed him and dragged him into the courtyard of the apartment building. Straining from the window to see what was happening, Larissa peered out in time to see the flash of light and hear the blast of the gun as her father was executed for all the neighbors to see. Later in life she would learn that he had spoken a word of truth to Stalin, a word that was, quite obviously, not well received. For his loyalty and sacrifice, he was made an object lesson for the community. The leaders still courted her mother, urging the family to move into the new apartment building. Her mother refused and from that time set a course for her girls to survive. Every acquaintance that took up the offer of the new apartment building was eventually executed.

The Great Patriot War against the Fascists, known in the West as World War II, impacted all of life in the Soviet Union. Because her mother had refused the generous offer of the Communist leaders, she was sent to the front to care for wounded soldiers. In an effort to save her girls, she took them to the Kievskiy train station and sent them off to Ukraine, where they were to stay with relatives for the duration of the war. Little did she know that within six weeks, that part of Ukraine would be overrun by German forces.

At first Larissa and her sister tried to imagine the war as some kind of adventure. Surely this would not last for long, and they would be able to go home and see their mother soon. The months became years, and their situation became dire. Little by little the food disappeared. While they were living on a farm, the soldiers would take everything, for they, too, were hungry. Faced with starvation, Larissa and her sister found a savior in a young German soldier named Hans. Every day he would drop by the farm and share some of his bread rations with the girls.

As the war raged on, all across the Soviet Union people were starving. The city of Leningrad was held under siege by the German army for 872 days. To this day the equivalent of two thin slices of bread is known as a "Leningrad portion"—the daily allowance of food for those captured in the city. Although they should have been blossoming into their teen years, the girls grew thin and gaunt, covered in lice. The number of casualties mounted to the millions. Men—fathers, brothers, uncles—would never come home again. The Soviet Union lost more people in the war than did all the other nations combined, and the scar across the landscape of the nation would last for generations.

The war finally ended, but there had been no communication between mother and daughters for years. It was presumed that the girls had died, when, much to her surprise, Larissa's mother received a telegram from Ukraine. The girls were alive and would be coming home to Moscow by train. Rushing to the Kievskiy station, this mother waited for the appointed train, but as she scanned the crowds disembarking, she could not find her girls. She was discouraged, thinking she had not received the correct information. At that moment, two straggly-looking young ladies ran to her, calling, "Mama." The war had taken such a toll on the girls that they were no longer recognizable to their own mother. After a moment of shock, they wept in a warm embrace—the girls were finally home.

Years later, Nazarene missionaries would move next door to Larissa and her husband, Timofei. Nearing election season in the 1990s, the old Communist Party was still out trying to find recruits and votes. The doorbell was rung for each apartment on the floor, and when Larissa opened her door, she spoke for all: "You murdered my father. Go away. We want nothing to do with you." This was a powerful statement from a woman who had married the secretary of the Moscow Communist Party during the time of Stalin. Timofei came from Ukraine to Moscow to serve the party. He and Larissa were brilliant young physicists and had helped to build a new Soviet Union after the war.

Communism was their religion. Lenin, the father of Soviet Communism, had often quoted Marx, saying, "Religion is the opiate of the people." Therefore, Communism embraced atheism, and religion was to be eradicated. The Russian Orthodox Church was severely marginalized and heavily infiltrated by the KGB. There had been a miracle, of sorts, in 1918, when in a six-month period, between the fall of the czar and the control of the Bolsheviks, Russia experienced democracy. In that small window of time, the Orthodox Church was able to elect a patriarch. There had not been a patriarch in Russia since the time of Peter the Great, when Patriarch Nikon had tried to extricate power from the czar. Peter took swift and decisive action against the church, removing the patriarch, replacing him with a synod, and forbidding the church to do any charitable work in the land. This would have a devastating and long-term impact on Christianity in this part of the world, which had embraced the faith since the year 988. Moscow had, at one time, been considered the third Rome, and even the double-headed eagle of Russia echoes the *aquila* (eagle) symbolism of the Roman Empire. This was the sacred space of Byzantium, the heart of Eastern Christianity after the sack of Constantinople, which was eventually brought down by greed. But in 1918, a ray of light broke through the darkness, and a patriarch rose to power. This was a leader who could help shepherd the church through a new season of oppression.

It is easy for Protestants to judge the Orthodox Church and its behavior during the seventy years of Communism. Many would say that the patriarch and the church compromised with government leaders, and in some ways, they did. However, the Orthodox Church is not a church that can go underground or become a house church. For the Orthodox Church to exist, the liturgy must be celebrated and chanted in the church every week. Without this public worship and liturgy, there is no church. Therefore, the leadership had to weigh the consequences between compromising with the government and the extinguishing of Christianity as they understood it.

Meanwhile, Protestant Christianity had existed before the revolution. The Salvation Army had a presence in Russia, as well as the Lutheran Church. Pentecostal groups and a homegrown group of believers had been flourishing. After the Bolsheviks came to power, they were determined to control religion. All of Christianity was organized into two groups: the Orthodox and the Union of Evangelical Christians-Baptists (UECB). The word "Baptist" became associated with all Protestants in the Soviet Union and was not an indicator of a Calvinistic theological perspective. These were the two major aboveground churches, while others chose to be unregistered and function underground.

The Cold War came on quickly as relationships between former allies became frozen in time. With the great losses faced by the Soviet Union there was a sense of destiny, or perhaps an entitlement, to some of the spoils of war. Eastern Europe came under the firm grip of the Soviet Union, with the Berlin Wall becoming the visible sign of a divided world. This political and physical division became known as the "Iron Curtain." Like male birds showing off for a potential mate, both East and West began building up enough armaments to destroy each other multiple times. In the meantime, people like Timofei had taken up the banner of Communism, ready to persecute Christians at a moment's notice. With his party responsibility came a list on Mondays of those who had attended church. Timofei was to determine their fate. Some might face a simple punishment, including loss of employment or ejection from education, but others were sent to Siberia and, potentially, to their death. This was a dangerous time, and many prayed that God would intervene to bring it to an end.

ONE

Item 15

FRANKLIN

I HAD TO RUSH to make my train—a TGV bound for Zurich. The TGV is one of France's spectacularly fast trains, going at speeds of up to two hundred miles per hour for commercial service. I had never been on a train so fast, so quiet, so well appointed. Paris has seven main train stations, and I was leaving from Gare de l'Est for the five-hour run to Zurich.

It was October 8, 1989, and I was excited. Settling in my luxurious seat as we left Paris, through the eastern suburbs and into the country, we quickly picked up speed. Soon, I was mesmerized by the blur of the French countryside, and my thoughts (train travel is a great venue for thinking) turned to the last two months. What was I doing on a speeding train between Paris and Zurich? Why was I here? The past two months had been a totally unexpected whirl of change, and now reality was setting in.

My mind went in reverse. I had a happy job working with business executives interested in church planting in Arizona and southern Nevada. I was also doing a "side job" as editor of *World Mission* magazine, a monthly promoting Nazarene global missions. In addition, Dr. Robert Scott, the global director at the time, had conscripted me to do "candidates." In the middle of that cascade of activity, Dr. Scott had dropped a bomb on me. I came to think of the bomb as "Item 15."

Dr. Scott was an organized man who made lists, created agendas, and always kept copious notes on a yellow legal pad. He had come to this position of leadership from a long and successful ministry in California, where I had met him years before. He and I met regularly in the interest of both the magazine and missionary candidates, and I could always count on a written agenda. In early August, we had one of our normal meetings, with fourteen items on the agenda.

Concluding the agenda, Dr. Scott leaned back in his chair and peered at me over his large wooden desk. Smiling but with intensity, and out of the complete blue, he shared "Item 15": "You have just been elected regional director of the Eurasia Region. Are you willing to consider it?"

Of all the shocks of my professional life, this was the largest. I was content living in Arizona and had no intention or desire to move. The possibility of moving to Europe would disrupt family, friends, lifestyle, my wife and her mother, in fact, just about everything I could think of. I am sure I just sat in my chair while blood drained to my feet. I think I stammered, "I will need to call Maylou." When I called her later that morning, I said, "How would you like to move to Europe?" to which she replied, "What have they offered you now?"

This plunged us into such things as vaccination shots at the public health office (they are cheaper there); police clearances to ensure we did not represent some criminal enterprise; applications for residency; the sale of a house; and decisions about what to take, what to keep, and what to store. At that moment, I had the sketchiest notions about what a regional director does or what the Eurasia Region encompassed. And I certainly did not have *any* idea what might lie ahead in that region. But over the next several weeks we received a repeated affirmation that this is what God wanted us to do. It meant a move to a so far unknown location, setting up an office, establishing residency, applying for permits and registration, and opening bank accounts. As I sat in my train seat, I wondered, "What have I gotten myself into?"

We had been mandated to move the office from Bolton, England, "to the Continent." When I asked where on the Continent, the answer was, "I don't know." We had no staff and little budget. My predecessor, Dr. Tom Schofield, was from England and a much-loved leader who had resigned suddenly on the advice of his doctors. I spent half a day with him reviewing ongoing issues on the region.

The Eurasia Region covered a vast geographical space, stretching from the Azores in the Atlantic to Siberia on the Bering Sea. It included all South Asia (India, Pakistan, etc.), the Middle East, Africa north of the Sahara, and everything on both sides of the Iron Curtain. I soon discovered that Europe was intensely complicated, not just by language but by history, culture, customs, and legacy. And behind the Iron Curtain were vast areas untouched and untouchable because of their subjugation since

World War II under Soviet Communism. These were places the Church of the Nazarene had never been.

When Dr. Scott brought up the unwritten agenda "Item 15," and when I eventually said yes to the invitation, I had no idea what lay ahead. It has often occurred to me that sometimes we are given the providence of ignorance—that God in his wisdom allows tomorrow to be a surprise. I have also often thought that had I known the future, I might not have had the courage to say yes.

On the train, watching the landscape blur past, I reflected on the complexity of the region. In its geography were housed the homes of three of the world's great religions: Christianity, Judaism, and Islam. It had given birth to many of the "isms" of the world, including Marxist Communism. It gave birth to the Renaissance, to the Reformation, to the Industrial Revolution, to the French Revolution, to the Russian Revolution, and so much more. It had over ninety countries, hundreds of official languages, and untold numbers of dialects. Stunning!

Running continually through my reverie was the question, "How did I arrive in this place at this time?" And then lunch arrived, a beautiful French lunch, served with panache and aplomb, at high speed. Here in this delectable repast was just some of what lay ahead in the great unknown.

And then, just five weeks after arriving in the region, November 9, 1989, happened. The world changed. I was in Amman, Jordan, trying to sleep at the Regency Palace Hotel. The day had been long and taxing. We had been in meetings that were not tranquil. I wanted to sleep but couldn't do more than toss and turn. Finally, I flipped on the television, an old black-and-white model mounted high in one corner, and saw something very curious and unnerving. People were climbing on a wall with hammers and chisels, pounding, chipping, and singing. I recognized the infamous Berlin Wall that had severed the city in two for decades, with the eastern side of the wall controlled by the Soviet Union and the western side by the allied powers (United States, Britain, France). I watched in fascination, and it dawned on me that this changed everything—everything, including my job description. The collapse of the wall meant the balance of power in the world had changed. New possibilities had opened for the church not just in the Soviet Union but also in the Middle East and South Asia. It meant the client states of Eastern Europe were rising in freedom and were also a possibility. It was an overwhelming moment that kept me sleepless for the balance of that night.

What was I to do? What was the church to do? What was the Eurasia Region to do? How would, or could, we respond to this burgeoning access to vast new areas for ministry? We were hardly prepared to open an office. How could we imagine opening new countries to the work of a church?

A few days later, after consulting with our German leaders, I sent out a call for a Berlin summit. The idea was to gather a group of decision-makers, visionaries, and people with resources to congregate in one place and begin a dialogue on the future. And they came. They came from Nazarene Headquarters representing youth, education, large local churches, and strategists. Even Dr. Scott, with his list of agenda items, was there. About thirty of us gathered. This was the big news of the times, and people wanted to help in any way they could. As we gathered to pray, talk, and strategize, everyone realized the enormity of the challenge. Already the two local Berlin Nazarene churches were in full gear, welcoming people from eastern Germany who had not been allowed to travel for decades, passing out soup, German bread, and coffee to hungry people—offering words of hope and spiritual encouragement. But along with these leaders of the denomination and of Europe was the "elephant in the room," the Soviet Union. It had been a foe. It was large. It was the mystery of Mother Russia.

And yet, with God's help, out of that room came a plethora of ideas, a commitment to gather financial and other resources, and a sense of unity in purpose. This was one of the largest challenges the church had ever taken on. But what none of us really understood was that this was coming at us, not we at it. Events were moving with such speed that we could only respond as intelligently as we were able. We were swimming in ignorance because we had never done this before on such a scale.

I fought with myself to avoid the paralysis of obstacles that seemed to stack up. We had no money, no budget, no personnel, no real knowledge of the languages (including Russian), no experience in engagement with the history and legacy of Eastern Orthodoxy, no experience dealing directly with Communist philosophy or ideals or atheism. But here is the miracle. As time passed, it seemed to me that each "obstacle" found an answer. Money arrived, unsolicited, from donors and churches; volunteers began to show up in abundance; books were read, and research was done on the whys and the hows; and even Nazarene colleges jumped in with teams, including the highly regarded Love Works program of Point Loma Nazarene University in California. There were also five single guys from

Southern Nazarene University who went to Bulgaria to carve out some Bible studies and lay the foundation.

Maylou and I would often sit in the evening and, either in spoken word or in silence, wonder, "How in this wide world did we end up amid all this chaos, stress, excitement, and unexplored territory?"

Item 15, huh?

TWO

A Walk around Red Square

FRANKLIN

IT WAS SEPTEMBER 1991, and I was back in Moscow for my second visit. This time there would be church leaders joining me for a series of meetings with Russian officials.

It was early morning, and I was eager to get out of the infamous Intourist Hotel, where we were staying. Walking up the street on a beautiful morning, I soon came to Red Square, considered to be one of the most historic squares in the world, located in the center of Moscow and at the center of government and cultural power in the nation.

Red Square has existed since the fifteenth century and has served as a market, a place for celebrations and demonstrations; it is almost mythical in its eight-hundred-thousand-square-foot size. With the variety of buildings, walls, monuments, and churches, it can bring joy or awe or strike fear.

On this September morning as I stepped into the square, I was struck by the cacophony of Soviet life during a year when the union was crumbling and a new Russia emerging. My eyes went to the huge mausoleum containing the gray embalmed body of Lenin, considered the father of the Soviet Union. There were a smattering of Russians paying homage to his cultlike memory. My eyes shifted to the enormous walls of the Kremlin, seat of the czars and now the Soviet government.

Also visible was the 1561 Saint Basil's Cathedral, a spectacular architectural achievement and the best known of the buildings around the square. Built during the time of Ivan the Terrible, it remains legendary. History tells us that Czar Ivan called in the architect and asked him if he could reproduce this beautiful church. When the architect responded in the affirmative, Ivan had his eyes gouged out; Ivan wanted Saint Basil's to be one of a kind. In past centuries, it had been a place of private worship for the czar and his family. At the time of the Bolshevik Revolution, its leading priests, along with thousands of others, were executed, and later in the fervor to destroy any religious influence, the building was slated for destruction. Only providence and a couple of architects saved the building until cooler heads prevailed.

On my walk, I came to the largest of the buildings, now called GUM (I will spare the reader the long official name in Russian), which had become the representative shopping location of the centralized economy of the country.

But what caught my greatest attention that morning were two preachers. What they were doing would have brought arrest and retribution just a year before. In one corner of Red Square, right by the intersection of GUM and the State Historical Museum, standing on a wooden box, was an American preacher with a megaphone, screaming at the top of his voice to the few who were listening to a sermon. I could tell that he was from the state of Texas, part of a virtual invasion of evangelical preachers who had come to this Cold War foe and atheist nation to bring the good news.

Standing in front of the museum, perhaps one hundred feet away, was a Russian Orthodox priest adorned in full regalia, also standing on a box, but with a microphone and a scratchy sound system, preaching at the top of his voice. It was a jarring moment listening to two preachers—one a Protestant from Texas in English, the other from Eastern Orthodoxy in Russian—speaking freely in Red Square, where any vestige of religious demonstration had been strictly prohibited since the 1917 Bolshevik Revolution.

After listening to the sermons for a few minutes, I strolled across the square to Saint Basil's past monuments and places where executions had frequently occurred under the czars through the centuries and under the Bolsheviks against dissidents who spoke a word against the Supreme Soviet State.

Spotting a major street leading away from the square, I strolled on until I came to a building I recognized. It was the notorious Lubyanka building, noted as the location of a prison run at the time by the KGB, now the FSB. Rumors, stories, and even jokes surrounded this building, the early parts of which were built in 1898. It was where dissidents went to be "interrogated." It was where judgments were issued and some individuals were sent off to the gulags of Siberia. It was a place to be avoided at all costs.

In front of the prison a large statue of Felix Dzerzhinsky had been erected. "Iron Felix," as he was often called, had been a revolutionary figure, born in 1877. He was arrested often by the czarist government, exiled to Siberia, eventually to join Lenin's Bolsheviks. He was named the head of the secret service in 1917 and engaged immediately in organized mass executions and systematic torture. He died in 1926 of a heart attack and was honored by Joseph Stalin as a hero of the state. Thus, the large statue.

However, on that September morning of my walk, I noticed that the statue was gone and all that remained was the plinth on which it had sat. In the revolutionary environment of 1990 and 1991 when thousands of statues were taken down, Iron Felix was toppled in August 1991. Here I was, one month later, at the plinth. But my interest was in an elderly man, walking around and around the plinth in circles, mumbling, yelling, and most notably spitting. I came closer, enough that he saw me. He knew some English and spoke to me in an agitated voice about the work of the KGB, the horrors of the prison, and the gulags of Siberia and told me that several of his relatives had been massacred through the years by the "system." But now there was "freedom," and he was celebrating by cursing and spitting in front of Lubyanka.

I had enough. I made my way back to the Intourist Hotel, while reflecting on the microcosm I had seen that early morning before appointments and meetings were to begin. I had seen the Kremlin, representing the immense power of the state; the embalmed body of Lenin, the founder of the Soviet Union; GUM, representing the economic system of a controlled command economy; Saint Basil's, representing the persecution of religion;

two contrasting preachers now free to preach; and Lubyanka, representing torture and imprisonment at a time of dramatic change.

It was enough to boggle the mind, to stir up the deepest of emotions, and to raise profound questions of just how we would bring the organization of the Church of the Nazarene to this ancient and troubled land. How indeed!

THREE
Rumblings

CARLA

THE MAJOR CHANGE in our lives occurred in October 1991, when out of the blue, my husband, Chuck, and I were asked by the head of the World Mission Department of the Church of the Nazarene, Bob Scott, whether we would move to Russia as missionaries. We were attending an evangelism conference in Fort Worth and were excited about what we were learning and how we could put it into practice in our local church in Austin. Before the final service began, in the lobby of the hotel, Dr. Scott asked if we might pray about moving to Russia. What? We had not applied for missionary service and were enjoying the ministry in Texas. That night we walked the streets of Fort Worth and sobbed like babies. We were overwhelmed that God would ask us to be involved in such a daunting task. However, in our hearts, we knew that we would be going to Moscow. Nothing would ever be the same again.

Moving to Russia was both exciting and overwhelming. The Lord's presence was so real, and only in the confidence that this was his will could we have ever gone. Those first years in Russia were to become the most challenging in our lives.

The first couple of months we lived in a hotel/hostel called the Bittsa. It would take time, and the assistance of a friend, Dr. Kent Hill, to find an apartment in which to live. Housing had been a problem in the Soviet Union, and the Communist government promised a living space to all their citizens. The allotted amount was a minimum of sixty square feet per person, so families often were brought together to live in communal apartments, sharing bathroom and kitchen facilities. Now, with the end of the Soviet Union, all apartments were privatized. Wherever you were assigned to live on a particular day, this became your personal property and could be legally bought, sold, and/or rented. Most people had no idea what it meant to be a landlord, but they did figure out that if they moved in with relatives and rented out their apartments to foreigners, they just might make enough money to support their families. By the end of the summer, we would be able to move into a two-bedroom apartment just off Leninsky Prospect, near Moscow State University. Having two bedrooms for our little family of four people was considered a luxury. We were a bit shocked to discover that all kitchen cabinets and appliances had been cleared out of the apartment before we arrived. There would be work to do! While this was a bit of a challenge, it was nothing compared to other missionaries who rented two-bedroom apartments, only to have their landlords ask for the return of one bedroom so that a "babushka" or grandma could live there.

The excitement in the global Church of the Nazarene about Russia was so great that even though there were no missionaries in the country, there were already four Work and Witness teams in the country before we arrived. They were helping to work on the Baptist headquarters because the Church of the Nazarene was officially sponsored by the Baptist Union. The teams also stayed at the Bittsa. Every night, team members would come back to the hotel and share about the people they had met and all the things we could do to minister there. They would want to take us and introduce us to different people. Sometimes we felt like failures because we didn't have the energy to go and meet all these people. We were living in a hotel—with no hot water, a broken toilet seat, and no laundry facilities. The night we arrived I had learned that the restaurant had closed down because they couldn't find enough food. At the front desk they had two cans of Cuban pineapple juice for sale, and that was all they had left.

The greatest gift to us was that of teammates and partners in ministry. Roy and Caroline Campbell had arrived before us in Moscow to coordinate the Work and Witness teams. These faithful laypersons had committed to serve the Lord wherever that might be. They had thought they were going to the Philippines after the summer, but we were hopeful that God had other plans in mind for them.

Roy Campbell had been a firefighter in Kansas City. In 1981, there had been a terrible accident at a hotel where 114 people died. Roy was one of the first rescue workers on site, helping to save hundreds of lives. Because of that accident, Roy's perspective on life changed, and after retiring as a firefighter, he and his wife, Caroline, committed their lives to serve the Lord on the mission field. Their first day in Moscow, Roy realized he needed to find a way to get around town. An official cab was difficult to find, but most anyone with a vehicle was willing to drive you across town for the right price. He watched and learned as he saw others put out their hand to the road and flag down a car. Soon he decided he would try this as well, and a light-colored Lada pulled to the side of the road. Inside was a young man named Misha, who just happened to speak some English. Just maybe it was the grace of God and an answer to prayer that arranged the meeting of Roy and Misha that day, for what developed was a lifelong friendship. Misha was an unemployed engineer, and he became a partner in construction and leading Work and Witness teams. The Campbells left at the end of that first summer, and we wept as we left them at the airport. We were grateful that they were able to return just a couple of months later, remaining on the field for two years.

Nazarene Youth International (NYI), led by Fred Fullerton, was committed to helping open the work in the former Soviet Union. David Bowser from the NYI office brought his family and moved into the Bittsa hotel. He came to lead the more than one hundred young people who volunteered to come that first summer. Feeding all these volunteers was a real challenge. They had been told to bring enough snacks in their luggage for their lunches, but that their supper would be provided. David was partnering with Roy to take care of all the volunteers. Hyperinflation was kicking in as the Russian ruble was left to float on the market. In January 1992, the exchange rate had been one ruble to one United States dollar, but by June, it was more than two hundred rubles to the dollar. The local currency would lose value from the morning to the afternoon, and so money would have to be exchanged at least twice a day. As inflation blew through the summer, shopping bags of cash were often needed to pay for meals and hotel bills. An arrangement was made with a local disco that had a restaurant. If we brought them cash in the morning, they would spend the day searching for food and feed dinner to our teams in the evening. In that way, one hot meal a day was provided for those who had sacrificed to come to Russia that summer. It was also another moment of prevenient grace, for we got to know Tanya Arakcheeva, a young waitress in the restaurant.

Near the end of that first summer, nearly every NYI president from across the United States and Canada came to Russia to see the opportunities for ministry. The church was being mobilized to engage in a mission field that just five years previous would have been unimaginable. Another member of the team, Hermann Gschwandtner, had a plan for reaching the entire former Soviet Union, made up of nearly four hundred million people, with the gospel. Hermann lived in Germany and was coming alongside Franklin Cook in the regional office. Working with Nikolaj Sawatzky, also from the regional office, he developed a concept called "literature evangelism." The plan was to introduce Christ to people, lead them into a life of faith, and enable them to meet in fellowship. Hermann developed *The Story of Jesus the Nazarene*, mostly derived from the gospel of Luke. A second book was *Life with Jesus the Nazarene*, which included how to live as a Christian, and a third was *The Way of Jesus the Nazarene*, which explained to the readers how they could start house churches in their homes without the need of a pastor or missionary. These were attractive paperback books, and they all concluded with an invitation to write to an address in Moscow to learn more about the Nazarene. This literature evangelism would eventually influence some of the initial work with the *JESUS* film in South Asia, and all told, 1.5 million copies of these different booklets were eventually printed in twenty different languages.

The Soviet Union had placed a great emphasis on literacy, with nearly 98 percent of society now literate and voracious readers. Every entrance to the subway system was littered with salespeople, hawking the latest books, alongside Western cigarettes and Russian vodka. Knowing that these books would be of interest, an order was made for four hundred thousand copies of the first volume. A semitruck arrived at the Bittsa hotel with hundreds of shrink-wrapped bundles of *Jesus the Nazarene*. It took hours to move them all into the volunteers' hotel rooms, this being the only storage space available. Suddenly, every room had end tables and coffee tables of *Jesus the Nazarene*. Some had them stacked to the ceiling, and all of us were wondering how we could get them distributed. We were able to find large bags for ice hockey equipment that we could load with hundreds of books. The NYI presidents would then take these bags down to the entrance to the subway stations and begin handing out books. We soon learned that it wasn't going to be difficult to give these books away. People lined up to get a free book, and a thousand books would disappear in a matter of thirty minutes.

One of the NYI leaders misunderstood the instructions. They were to only go to the entrance to the subway, not into the subway system itself. Suddenly, this individual was separated from his partner and in a place where he was not to have been. Every subway station has its own police station where the "militsiya" have an office. This poor soul found himself face-to-face with a member of the "militsiya" who took him away and into the police holding area. He later recounted that his life flashed before his eyes as he wondered whether he would ever see his family again. No one knew where he was, and he had no way of communicating with the police. They were trying to talk to him, but he was paralyzed with fear. Finally, after what seemed to be an eternity, but was probably about an hour, he understood the word "dollar." Ah—maybe they were just wanting a little "tip." A ten-dollar bill was pulled from the pocket, and that seemed to do the trick. Our NYI president was set free, but he returned to the Bittsa shaken and looking for a different assignment on the subsequent days of his visit. In the meantime, thousands of books were delivered into the hands of the people, and the gospel was spread. We would have to wait and see if anyone would write to the address. Teammates in ministry, missionaries and volunteers came and went through the years, but they were always there when needed, as agents of God's grace.

Having come from the comforts of the West, adjusting to daily life was a challenge. There were only two restaurants in this city of ten million that had food on a regular basis: McDonald's and Pizza Hut. Many days were spent trying to find something for our family to eat that could be cooked in our little hotel room on a hot plate. We learned early on that the local restaurants were unpredictable. After taking a group of visitors to a fine-looking hotel restaurant, we would peruse the menu. When the waiter would come, the first guest might request an item off the menu, only to be told, "We don't have that today." Moving on to a second choice, the guest would be told, "We don't have that today either." After discovering that none of the choices were available, we would ask, "What do you have?" "Oh, today we only have chicken Kyiv." This happened regularly, and it became comical as we wondered why we were handed a full menu when there was barely any food in the kitchen.

Doing laundry for a family of four was another thing. There were no Laundromats, and few people had a washing machine, let alone a dryer. There were nights that our fingers would bleed from doing our washing by hand in a freezing cold shower in the hotel. You may wonder why the water was freezing cold. In the Soviet system, everything was centralized, even the heat and hot water. The city of Moscow had six cogeneration plants, where water was heated to produce steam and thus electricity, and the residual hot water was sent throughout the city to heat homes and provide hot water for the taps. However, in the summer, when heating wasn't necessary, the plants would be shut down, one at a time, to do maintenance and repairs. When your plant was shut down, there would be no hot water for up to a month. This was just part of the normal rhythm of life during the Soviet days. We assumed that people took cold showers in these summer months, and it would take us until our second summer to realize that the Russian people had a way of dealing with the system. By that time, we learned that the first adult up in the morning would put a pot of water on the stove to heat. In the meantime, a very large mixing bowl was placed in the bottom of the tub. This would be filled half-full of nearly boiling water, and then cold water would be added until it was just the right temperature. One could stand in the tub and use a large cup to shower or bathe with nice warm water. Each pot would take care of two people. If four people needed to bathe, you just repeated the process. But that first summer, we weren't that smart, and we didn't have a bathtub. The hotel only had a shower, and so we stood in the cold water, rubbing those little socks together, trying desperately to get them clean.

We were just trying to survive, and yet amid it all, we were supposed to be missionaries bringing people to Christ! Some days we didn't feel as if we were good Christians or missionaries, because we were in survival mode. Finally, at the end of the summer, all the Americans left, and we had to pull things together and begin a church.

FOUR

Church and State

FRANKLIN

LOOKING AT THE HISTORY OF RELIGION in Russia is like examining a spiderweb. Intricate connections and relationships, ideas and conflicts, reach back through a murky history. It was in the year 988 when Vladimir the Great opted for a form of Christianity that had been declared the official religion of the Byzantine Empire. The citizens of the Byzantine Empire at the time considered themselves Romans and part of the Eastern Roman Empire. The imperial seat of power had moved from Rome to Byzantium, where Greek rather than Latin was the predominate language. The Byzantine Empire lasted from AD 330 to AD 1453, with its center in Constantinople (today's Istanbul). Much later, in the nineteenth century, Czar Nicholas I proclaimed, "Orthodoxy, autocracy, and nation." In other words, to be Russian meant loyalty to the czar and adherence to Russian Eastern Orthodoxy.

Through its long and often dark history, the splits, factions, disputes, and oppression of religion led to a perplexing landscape in the competition for the soul of Mother Russia. Combined with the medieval traditions, fostered and nurtured by the absolute political power of the czarist governments, church and state were often blended without distinction or boundaries. Until 1905, by law, only the Russian Orthodox Church was allowed to engage in the missionary work of conversion. Conversely, no other religious tradition was allowed to proselytize in any way (though, of course, they did, covertly).

At the same time, there existed elements of the Roman Catholic Church and Lutheranism brought to the country largely by German immigrants, imported en masse by Catherine the Great (who herself had been a German princess before marriage and who ruled with an iron hand as czarina from 1762 to 1796) to develop agriculture along the great Volga River and adjoining plains. She promised the Germans one hundred years of tax-free living in German colonies. They would serve as a human barrier between the Mongols and the rest of Russian society, but they were free to farm, worship, and retain their life and culture.

In the mid to late eighteenth century, Karl Marx, one of the fathers of Communism, stated that "religion is the opiate of the people," meaning that religion's role is as a "metaphysical balm" for the real suffering both in the universe and in society. This was a foundational aspect of the 1917 Revolution overthrowing the czarist regime and installing a new "proletariat" of governance that elevated the state to be the supreme power and worked to eradicate religion from the nation. Priests and pastors were to be killed, monasteries closed, religious symbols, even the Holy Bible, were to be controlled by the state, with the goal of eliminating the opiate of God from society. There was to be a "new man," the Soviet ideal, under the symbol of the hammer and sickle. The hammer representing workers together with the sickle representing peasants was to be plastered on walls, auditoriums, flags, and banners, all under a single red star.

So, in the 1991 upheaval, which overthrew the Soviet system through coup, intrigue, and manipulation, and the ensuing chaos, suddenly religious expression became a possibility. And in came a flood of information about the Bible, religion, and church, including the Church of the Nazarene. But the question was, How does a religions organization achieve legal recognition? No one really knew.

The deceased longtime dictator, Joseph Stalin, had brutally enforced regulations against all forms of religious life. However, in 1944 when Russia was on the verge of losing in its battle with Germany in the Great Patriotic War, Stalin decided to seek the support of all the cults and fringe groups by forcing all religious factions to "voluntarily" join the Union of Evangelical Christians-Baptists (UECB).

Dr. Hermann Gschwandtner, Nazarene pastor and leader in Germany, had for years been working for Every Home for Christ as continental director for Eastern Europe and had made many contacts with Christian leaders in the East. Among these were leaders from UECB, and so naturally, to them he turned when conditions changed. Suddenly, it appeared that there would be a possibility of reaching agreements with officials of both church and state.

From 1991 through 1992, there were meetings with small groups of Nazarene leaders and leaders of the Ministry of Cults (an agency of the Soviet system designed to monitor and control any religious group that was not a part of the Orthodox

Church). I was involved in several of these meetings, all of which were memorable to say the least.

One meeting was in a dark and crowded office of a deputy secretary of the Ministry of Cults, a middle-aged man who represented the Soviet establishment. I posed for him, during the meeting, what seemed to me to be a perfectly normal question on behalf of the church. "What are the procedures for securing residence visas and work permits for religious workers?" I asked. I remember him leaning back in his chair, bursting out with a smirk, and declaring, "We have no procedures for this. The reality is, no one wants to come to work in Russia—they only want to leave." He knew he was about to lose his job, since the Soviet government was disintegrating at that very moment. There were no procedures. We sat in awkward silence. So, how were we to register?

Nonetheless, in a separate meeting, we did make an agreement with the UECB in a Memorandum of Understanding (MOU) for them to become a sponsoring agency for the Church of the Nazarene to operate legally (although those laws changed in a matter of weeks under a new government, which eventually became the Russian Federation). This happened on January 30, 1992.

Later, other measures were taken to find ways of securing visas, and even a procedure for the purchase of property in a society where for three quarters of a century, no personal ownership of property had been allowed. It proved to be a challenging legal process that continues even to this day, as the government tries to discourage the free expression of religion.

Dr. Kent Hill encouraged the Sunbergs to work with a Russian attorney, Natalia Visotskaya. A believer, she had been tapped by Chuck Coleson to lead his prison ministry in Russia. There were a myriad of legal questions and concerns. After a lengthy sit-down with this deeply thoughtful woman, the Sunbergs were left with a dilemma. She had explained that the Soviet laws had been written in such a way that a person would always be breaking them. There was no way to function within the law, because they were set before you as a trap. That way, the government could always have an excuse to arrest you. The best she could do was give advice on what might be the way forward, with the caveat that there was never really a "right" answer. This led to some real soul-searching when it came to making decisions. When one comes from a society of law and order, the idea of having to make personal judgment calls on a daily basis was to become a source of stress for the Sunbergs. Even the World Mission policy manual was of little help because the church had never worked in this kind of society before. It was all new and a little terrifying.

Interestingly, it was discovered that in Soviet law, the government could not take housing from a woman with children. Although the World Mission policy manual said that missionaries were not to buy property or hold it in their own names, on the advice of our Russian attorney, eventually all apartments were held in the names of our female missionaries who had children. This, however, led to another challenge, since every time our missionaries left the country to renew their visas (which was sometimes once or twice a year), they would have to reregister in their places of residence. Even when the female missionary owned the apartment, she would have to go to the local authorities within three days to get permission for her family to live in the home with her. A letter had to be written with the request for the family members to be registered in the home. The first encounter at the government office would be with the office of utilities to see whether all bills had been paid. There were no meters, but the charges for utilities were based on the number of individuals registered to live in the housing unit. If there was an outstanding sum, the bill would have to be paid before the requested permission would be granted. The bill could not be paid at the government office, but at a local bank in cash, with the bank receipt properly filled out in Russian. If the receipt was not filled out perfectly, the individual behind the window would scream at the person trying to pay the bill, probably tell the person that he or she was stupid, and send him or her to the back of the line. It might take hours to pay the utility bill, only to finally return to the government office with the completed receipt. This, however, would only gain one access to the next window.

On one occasion, Carla Sunberg was stopped by the head of the precinct, who was to give the final approval for her family to live with her, and asked how many radiators she had in her apartment. Quickly, she counted in her head and provided what she thought was the right answer. Then he asked her if they were the original radiators or if they had ever been changed or upgraded. Actually, they had been changed because they were in such poor condition. He asked whether the Sunbergs had paid to have the water shut off so that the radiators could be changed out. They had not paid to have the water shut off, because they changed them during the time of the year when the water is already shut off by the government to do work on the pipes, usually about a month every summer. Carla was then told that this was not fair. It was not fair for them to change the radiators when the water was already off and not pay to have the water turned off. She would have to return to her apartment with a city engineer who would count her radiators so that she could be charged for turning off the water that didn't need turning off. If she did not do this, her family could not be registered to live in her home. After another few hours of radiator counting and fine paying, at the end of the day, all the Sunbergs were allowed to live together in the home that they owned.

The greatest challenge to navigating the legal system was the breakup of the Soviet Union. The Sunbergs' very first visas came through the UECB and were for the Soviet Union. Within a month of the Sunbergs' arrival, borders were being established between the newly independent states. Each new country had to write its own laws and determine a process for obtaining visas. If a person traveled from Moscow to Kyiv, he or she might still be in the same country, or maybe not. Who knew! Sometimes, it was obvious—only the Lord knew.

FIVE

First Works

CARLA

THROUGHOUT THE FIRST SUMMER, the Youth in Mission teams, as well as the Work and Witness teams, had made contacts with young people in the community. Russia has long summer nights, and staying up and enjoying the respite from winter is thoroughly embraced, with bedtime around midnight. As a result, each evening people would mill around the outdoor arena at the Bittsa sporting complex where we were staying. The Americans would bring out their baseball gear and begin to play. Young people would gather around and ask to join in, and soon, a crowd would gather. They were there to play, try out their English, and ask these young volunteers what had brought them to Russia. A similar group of volunteers had also made their way to Ukraine, and the scene was repeated each evening in the city of Kyiv.

Curiosity not only about Americans but also about the Bible and Christianity was rife among the people we were meeting. The Bible had been confiscated from many homes, and now, suddenly, people were free to read it and discuss its contents. After seventy years of secrecy, people wanted to know why there had been such fear of this book. The hunger for information and spiritual things was great and continued to grow among the young adults who had now found themselves free to peruse Christianity.

Many of the Russian young people came out to tell the volunteers goodbye. The rented bus appeared, and the people and bags were loaded. We stood there with our new friends, waving goodbye to those who had served so well that summer. There were tears in our eyes, for we would miss the new friends we had made, but they were also for our little family who was waving goodbye to our last connection to "home." We would now be on our own, with the Campbells and Mark Mann, a young member of the summer teams, not coming back for a couple of months. We were still living in the hotel.

Somehow the Lord got us through those first few months. That first weekend, after the teams left, we gathered the Russian young people at the hotel and had a conversation about what we ought to do next. We asked them if they would like to begin church services, and they all said yes. Having studied some missiology, Chuck and I didn't want to put too much of our personal imprint on the church. There were very few Protestant churches in the country, and yet we didn't want to plant an American church, but rather one that reflected the local context. We began to ask questions, trying to get ideas from these young people about "how" to do church. Finally, one of them spoke up and said, "We've never been in a church in our lives. We have no idea what church is supposed to be like." So together we began to dream about a brand-new Church of the

Nazarene in the former Soviet Union. Volunteers Jim and Donna Welchley were having similar conversations with the young leaders in Kyiv. The beginnings of a church in the former Soviet Union were taking form.

In Moscow, we rented a hall, right by the Bittsa hotel, where we could have services on Sundays. The entire Bittsa complex had been built for the equestrian events of the 1980 Olympics. The facilities had seen better days, but the staff was willing to allow us into their auditorium, complete with grand piano and speaker's podium. It seemed like the perfect fit. The young people gathered on Saturday to practice songs they had learned from the college students over the summer. One or two could play the guitar, others sang, and enough spoke English that we could communicate. Vladimir would become Chuck's translator. News spread by word of mouth that we would have our first church service at the end of August, and that first Sunday nearly fifty people came, maybe out of curiosity, but also to learn about that which had been hidden for so long. The response was enthusiastic, and they wanted to continue, and so we met, week after week, praying that the Spirit of God would be moving among these seekers.

The first winter, we learned that it would be a couple of months before the heat was turned on. The government waited until it had become sufficiently cold before they would fire up the heat in those cogeneration plants. Snow was already falling in September. Our oldest daughter, Christy, started kindergarten at the Anglo-American school, and a note was sent home to all the parents, informing them that children do not stay inside for recess during the winter but would need to be dressed appropriately. Outdoor boots would need to be worn to school, and indoor shoes provided. The only time that school would be closed was when it became minus forty-five degrees Celsius (without windchill), and this was because the public buses would no longer run because the diesel fuel would thicken and begin to gel. Dressing for school was like preparing to go out skiing for the day, with multiple layers of clothing, mittens and/or gloves, and a snowsuit, all topped off with a warm hat. Inside the apartment it grew colder and colder, as we anticipated the day the heat would be turned on. The long underwear came on in September and became a staple until May. The situation at the rented hall for church was no better. The girls would cry because they were so cold, and I tried to play the piano with gloves on. The Russians consider it a great victory when a foreigner can survive one of their winters. We did survive. In fact, we didn't just survive; we began to thrive.

Not long after our arrival, Chuck was asked to become the field director for the work in the former Soviet Union. At this point that simply meant Moscow and Kyiv, but it also meant a vision for what God might want to do across this vast field. The volunteers in Kyiv, Jim and Donna Welchley, headed back home, and the field was in transition. Chuck headed down to Kyiv to prepare the way for the arrival of new missionaries, David and Shelly Hayes and family. He would ride the train for fourteen hours, but before he left, he prayed that the Lord might use him to touch someone's life in a special way. Nothing unusual happened on his trip down, and he was able to accomplish all that he anticipated during his time in Kyiv. He had almost forgotten about his prayer when he boarded the train for the return trip to Moscow. Walking down the narrow hallway of the train, Chuck found his compartment, a coupé designed for four individuals, with two seats on the bottom and two bunks that would pull out to create upper berths at night. He was assigned one of the upper berths.

The other passengers, two men and a woman, eventually made their way into the compartment. They were speaking Russian with one another and then turned to speak with Chuck. He spoke very little Russian at this point and so responded in English. The pretty blond-haired woman perked up and spoke to him in English. They were very curious why an American might be on the train with them. As the conversation continued, he shared about his work and why he had been in Kyiv. The discussion shifted to the border crossing, which they would be approaching around midnight. Just a few months ago, there had been no border between Russia and Ukraine; it had all been one country, the Soviet Union. Our visas were for the Soviet Union, and now the newly independent states were regularly setting up border crossings and establishing their own visas. We never knew when this would happen and how it would impact our travel. If you lived in Moscow, you would have to get a new passport for the Russian Federation. If you lived in Kyiv, you would have to get a Ukrainian passport. What would happen when they reached the newly created border in the middle of the night? The greatest concern was for Chuck and how the border patrol would view his visa. Technically, we now had visas for a country that no longer existed. My passport said I also was born in a country that no longer existed (West Germany). Everything was changing quickly. Chuck made it over the border, but this would be the last time he would be able to travel to Kyiv without a Ukrainian visa.

Tamara was the lady in the train compartment that night. She had traveled to Kyiv to see her ailing mother and in desperation had gone to an Orthodox church to see if there was a priest who could pray for her. She was shocked to discover that the Orthodox church had a menu available with prices for religious services. She would have to pay for someone to pray for her mother. A faithful Communist and atheist, Tamara was now desperate to help her mother. The health-care system had fallen apart, and there were no medications, and she had lost all hope. As she and Chuck talked on into the night, he began to wonder if there was someone in Kyiv or Moscow that he could contact who could pray for this woman and her mother. Suddenly, it was as if the Lord spoke to him and said, "You can pray for her!" He looked at her and said, "I can pray for you and your mother." She burst into tears, wondering how she had ended up in this compartment with a Protestant "priest." He also assured her that his small church community in Moscow would pray for them as well. She asked if she could come and meet the people at the church. After explaining where the church was located, she was shocked. She only lived two metro stations from where the church was meeting at the Bittsa. It was then that Chuck understood that the Lord had answered his prayer before heading to Kyiv. Tamara was the answer to his prayer.

On Sunday, Tamara and her son arrived at the Bittsa sports complex and found the auditorium where we had church. Our new little church family welcomed them with open arms and, during the special time of prayer, surrounded them and prayed for them. Just a few weeks later, she and her son gave their lives to Christ and were the first two people to be baptized by the Church of the Nazarene in Russia.

Chuck got a call through to Franklin Cook, posing some questions about this new congregation. One question was about the offering. Should they begin taking an offering right away? How would it all be explained to the people? Franklin responded, "I don't know, but whatever you do, they will do it into the future." Having been a pastor in the United States, Chuck decided to talk to the people about tithing and about "paying budgets." After his first sermon on tithing, some of the older women came to him and asked him whether that was really in the Bible. He told them of course it is! Then they asked him why he hadn't told them sooner, because they wanted to do everything they were supposed to do to be faithful followers of Jesus. He challenged that local church to also tithe to the "budgets." Thus, from the first day they took offerings, they gave 5 percent to the World Evangelism Fund, 2.5 percent to the district, and 2.5 percent to the college fund. If you check the giving record for the districts in the former Soviet Union, you will see that they still pay their World Evangelism Fund in full. This became a part of the DNA of the Church of the Nazarene in that part of the world.

SIX

The Place of Prayer

CARLA

THE DAY WE LEFT FOR RUSSIA, Dr. and Mrs. Ralph Earle (one of Chuck's seminary professors) had come to the airport in Kansas City to see us off and to pray for us. They promised that they would pray for us every day that we were on the field. As long as they were mentally and physically able, they lifted us up to the Father. Within a few years, they both passed away. We knew that they had been praying for us every day, and we often wondered whether there were others who would pick up that mantle and continue to pray for missionaries. I don't think we can begin to imagine all that happens in the heavenly realm when God's people pray.

One night we had to drive to a city three hours from Moscow for an official meeting. A few of the folks from Moscow had gone with us, but as we prepared for the drive back, we were in for a rude awakening. The van died out on the highway, in the middle of nowhere. As the sun was setting in the distance, we were surrounded by a Russian forest of birches, dusted with a few firs here and there. We knew that we would need help getting to the next town, and so we ventured out on the road and tried to flag down a car. No one would stop. Finally, one of our Russian congregants, Sergei, traipsed into the woods and returned with a downed birch, about two meters in length. Then he marched out into the middle of the highway, tree in hand like a barrier, and stood his ground until the next vehicle stopped. He asked if they would tow us to the next town. Like every good Russian driver, we had a tow rope with us, and we were pulled to the next town, where we hoped we could find some help. Unfortunately, it was too late at night, so we looked for a way to get home to Moscow. We made our way to the train station, but there were no more trains to Moscow that night. Finally, we decided we would try and find a taxi that would drive us two hours to the city.

Our taxi, and that's being generous, was an old Lada with racy pictures plastered across the dashboard. We barely made it down the street when our driver pulled over at a public well to pump some water into a two-liter bottle and pour it into the engine. By now, it was pitch-black outside, and I was wondering whether anyone, besides me, was praying! As we made our way back to the highway, we had to pass a police checkpoint. There was a policeman in the road with his black-and-white striped baton, and he had his eye on our vehicle. We hadn't even made it to the open road, and we were already stopped. Chuck and I held our breath as our driver was taken from the car and interrogated by the policeman. Something was wrong with the documentation, and there was the threat that the vehicle might be confiscated. More prayer. Finally, the driver returned and said it was no big deal, and we headed down the road.

Soon the traffic was stalled on the highway. Something was wrong. A very long and large vehicle was pulled onto the road in front of us. Chuck and I looked at each other, and speaking in English said, "Was that an ICBM [intercontinental ballistic missile]?" And yes, it was. Eventually, as it was nearing midnight, we began moving. We drove another thirty minutes or so until we were stopped again at the next police checkpoint. After another lengthy conversation (and probably the exchange of some bribe money) with the policeman, our driver reappeared, and we continued what was turning into an incredibly long ride back to the city. We were next confronted with another traffic jam. There was an accident in front of us. As we made our way around the crumpled car, there was the body of a young woman on the road. No one had covered her, but it was obvious that she had perished. Is anyone praying? We made it as far as the next police checkpoint where our "luck" gave out. This time, our driver was unable to talk his way out of the situation. The car was confiscated, he was taken away, and we were left standing on the road at a police checkpoint at three in the morning. We found a phone and called a volunteer, Linda Russell, in Moscow. She came and found us looking rather pitiful on the side of the road and drove us home to our apartment. It was just before sunrise, but as we turned on the light in our bedroom, it exploded and caught fire. I didn't want to ask, "What else could happen?" But I certainly knew that we, and our work, needed to be bathed in prayer. It felt like a whole night of spiritual warfare, but by the grace of God, we had made it home.

Daily Bread

Jesus, when teaching us to pray, tells us that we are to pray for our daily bread. However, how many of us are truly concerned about finding bread every day? It's simple enough to go down to the supermarket and buy a loaf of bread. It's not that expensive, and it's filled with enough preservatives to last much longer than just a day! I believe that what Jesus is really telling us is that he wants us to be dependent on him for life's everyday needs. Unfortunately, when we have the means to supply our own needs, we don't think we need to rely on him. "Give us this day our daily bread" then simply becomes a nice line we say when we recite his prayer.

I had never experienced food shortages before in my life. It was easy enough to simply go to the store and buy whatever I needed. Suddenly, I was faced with the challenge of finding enough food to feed my family. My first trip to the bread store was quite an occasion. Roy and Caroline Campbell had already been there a few weeks, so they were trying to show us the ropes. We walked about a half a mile down the dusty sidewalk and through the knee-high grass until we finally arrived at the bread store. It looked as if several hundred people were milling around in and out of the store. I felt like a child again, as if it were my first day of school. I was scared to go inside, and I couldn't read a single sign. It all looked like Greek to me. At the entrance to the building, we found a bank of wooden doors, all locked shut, but one. My eyes had to adjust to the darkness as we stepped inside, and I nearly tripped over the metal grating, which I would learn later was used to clean the snow off your shoes in the winter.

There was something nostalgic about the store. Somehow it looked like a Norman Rockwell painting come to life. The center of the store was empty, but the walls were all lined with shelves, and in front of them were glass cases. The clerks stood behind the cases, and I noticed that there, under the glass, were just a few loaves of bread. Roy told me to follow him as he would teach me the process of purchasing bread. It was already a warm summer morning, and the humidity was climbing, along with the heat. Most of the people in line were women, dressed in sleeveless summer dresses and high-heeled shoes.

We found the end of the line and began to hold our position. I quickly realized that personal space was not an issue here, but maintaining your place in line was. A small amount of personal space would be considered a vacant position in line. It was important to keep pushing forward. Finally, we made it to the glass cabinet, and there before me were three loaves of bread: one white with two long cuts in the top, another white with diagonal cuts, and finally one very dark loaf. I didn't know what I was supposed to do. Roy quickly pointed to the white loaf with the diagonal cuts. The woman brusquely handed us a postage-stamp-size piece of butcher paper with a number written on it, and with that, she was done with us.

I was confused. I had no bread. All I had was a little piece of paper. I was afraid to ask Roy questions because although the building was full of people, it was also deathly silent. No one was talking to anyone, and I didn't know if I should speak out loud or not. I was afraid of them hearing me speak in English. Roy led me over to another line. This time when we reached the front, there was a woman standing behind a large gray manual cash register. She seemed to have a permanent scowl etched on her face. Roy handed her the piece of paper, along with some money. She grabbed the money rather angrily because she realized she would have to give him change. The scowl was now accompanied by a glare. She next whipped out an abacus the size of a washboard. I watched as her fingers flew over the abacus and then reached in the till to give us change and a receipt.

Nearly thirty minutes had passed since entering the store. We had a receipt, but we had no bread. I was silently following my leader, Roy, but now he led me back to the end of the original line. I was perplexed. What were we doing? However, Roy had a look of confidence on his face, and I was simply going to trust him. What else could I do? My senses were overloaded as I tried to absorb it all in the crush of people holding their positions in line. Strangely, amid all the sights, sounds, and odors, one smell was missing. It was that wondrous smell from Saturday afternoons when my mother used to bake bread; that smell that says, "You're home," or "You're safe here." The Communist system had consolidated all the bakeries, and all the bread was now baked in factories. The bread stores were simply distribution points, and they carried the same three varieties that every other bread store in town carried. While I was carried away in my thoughts, we had made our way back to the glass counter. We handed the woman our receipt, and she reached behind her with her bare hand and grabbed our unwrapped loaf of bread. We made our way to the door with our precious cargo, and when we reached the sunlight, Roy thrust the loaf of bread into the air, as if it were an Olympic torch and he had just won the marathon.

In the days ahead, I learned many lessons about shopping for bread. Many a day I ventured out on my own. I really did not like waiting in the lines, and I had discovered that later in the day, when I would peer in the door, the ladies in the store did not look very busy and there were no lines. I decided that I would outfox them and come in the afternoon, after the lines had gone down. Little did I know that the Communist system required the stores to remain open until evening, even if they had nothing to sell. No wonder the ladies in the store didn't look very busy! Every day they would run out of their supply of bread, and the rest of the day they would simply sit and chat with one another.

Our first winter began to set in, and along with winter came a plummeting economy. Now, even if there was bread to buy, many of the elderly could no longer afford it. Their buying habits began to change, and they would ask to purchase a quarter or a half loaf of black bread. My heart broke when I learned that the average retiree was now living on eight dollars a month, surviving on black bread and tea for days on end.

"Give us this day our daily bread." I had never truly understood this lesson, and it was one that I would learn well from my dear Russian friends. I would fall in love with the people and with their wonderful bread—bread made without any preservatives. If you didn't eat up your bread, it would begin to grow a blue-green mold within a couple of days. Just as the manna in the wilderness could not be collected and stored up, neither could the bread in Russia. We learned to be dependent on the Father to provide us with daily bread, and at the same time, we learned to be dependent on him for spiritual bread.

God doesn't promise to give us everything that we want, but he does promise to care for our needs. How much bread do we need? How much of anything do we need? "Give us this day our daily bread" is also a reminder or even a warning that we should not be stockpiling our personal and material possessions. In the fourth century, famine struck parts of the Roman world. Saint Basil the Great, trying to feed the poor, preached a sermon to those who were hoarding their wealth: "The bread that is spoiling in your house belongs to the hungry. The shoes that are mildewing under your bed belong to those who have none. The clothes stored away in your trunk belong to those who are naked."[1] The wealthy had more than enough, while the poor were starving.

I'm back in America now, and I can go to the supermarket and buy any type of bread I would like, and I don't even have to wait in line. I'm quite shocked that it can take weeks for the blue-green mold to appear! At the same time, I miss my Russian bread. And may I never forget what it truly means when we pray, "Give us this day our daily bread."

First-Century Flashbacks

When we arrived in Moscow, there was a lot of activity going on with mission groups, including ours. The Russian churches were trying to get connected with whomever they could for help with their ministries. It was a bit chaotic at first. Amid the chaos, we received a call one day from a Russian Baptist church in the town of Salekhard, way out in Siberia. They asked us if we would consider helping them evangelize the villages scattered up and down the Ob River. Since we were just starting

1. Quoted in Leonardo Boff, *The Lord's Prayer: The Prayer of Integral Liberation*, trans. Theodore Morrow (Maryknoll, NY: Orbis Books, 1983), 84, Internet Archive, https://archive.org/details/lordsprayerpraye0000boff/page/n7/mode/2up.

our work and asking God to lead us where he wanted us to go, we thought this would be a good thing to do. Besides, Chuck had never been to Siberia. Since they wanted us to come in July, Chuck thought, "Why not? There's no snow to deal with." We agreed to join them by sponsoring their evangelistic efforts. This was our second summer in the country. A Youth in Mission (YIM) team, sponsored by the World Mission Department, would come and join Chuck and the others. It would be a life-changing experience for them all.

The arrangements were made, and the group went to the airport to board their Yak-40. After much prayer they took off, heading northeast, to Siberia. Halfway there they landed to refuel and were then able to continue the rest of the way. As they were preparing to land, they looked out the window of the plane and discovered that the area surrounding the airport looked like an airplane cemetery. Old planes had been abandoned in this place. There were even remnants of a crash or two. Very encouraging. As they landed, the runway was very bumpy. When the group deplaned, they noticed that the runway was a sort of old grating, which, we surmised, must have been devised for better traction in the wintertime snow.

This was Chuck's first experience in the Siberian town of Salekhard. The town had a population of around thirty thousand, and it was a regional center. The team was met by some of the Baptist brothers with whom they would be partnering on this mission. They were told that the plan was to get on a boat in the morning and travel for about five hours before reaching the first village where they would do ministry. The boat was equipped with sleeping quarters and a galley, and this would become the home for the team for the next week.

There were seven in the group: three YIM students, one volunteer who was with us for the first year, two of our Russian sisters, and Chuck. In the morning, they boarded the boat and took off up the river. It was very warm, even hot at times. We learned that July is summer in Siberia. The people who live there year-round prefer the winter because there are no mosquitoes and it is easier to get around. Once everything is frozen over, they can drive on the rivers and lakes. The view along the river was breathtaking. The water was teeming with fish, and the land was wild and untouched.

Eventually, they arrived at the first village, which had around two hundred people living there. Some of the people were descendants of dissidents who were arrested by the government years before for being outspoken in their opposition to the government. Their punishment was to be exiled to a remote Siberian village. Others in the village were indigenous people called Nenets. They were called pagans by the other villagers. When the boat pulled up to the shore (there was no dock), a plank was lowered and the team made their way gingerly to land. They walked to the center of the village, and people started coming from everywhere. This group was quite the sight for them to see.

After getting organized, they introduced themselves, sang some songs, and Chuck preached a short message from John 3:16. He talked about Jesus. He told them that Jesus loved them and wanted them to be his followers and that Jesus could touch them at the point of their deepest need. At the end of the short message, the YIM team began making balloon animals for the children. They had never seen anything like that, and the reactions were priceless.

As Chuck stood there, watching it all happen, a little lady who was part of the indigenous population pulled on his shirt. He looked down at her, and there by her side was a small boy. She asked Chuck if he believed what he had just said, and he told her that he did. She asked him if it was all true, the person he was talking about, and Chuck said, "You mean Jesus?" She said, "Yes. Can this Jesus really help me with anything?" Chuck responded that he could. She looked at her small boy. She told Chuck that he was seven years old and had never spoken a word, and she asked, "Could Jesus touch him?" Chuck thought to himself, "OK, now this is serious." She had so much hope and even faith in her voice. She was desperate for her son. Chuck put his arm around her and her boy and prayed a simple prayer for him. When Chuck opened his eyes, nothing had happened with her son, but the woman was weeping. The tears were streaming down her face, and all she could say over and over was, "Spasibo, Jesus!" (Thank you, Jesus!).

Was this what it was like with the first-century disciples? Telling people the story about Jesus, people hearing his name for the first time, and people then believing? It was a powerful moment. About that time another lady came and said that she had something she wanted to show Chuck. One of our Russian sisters and Chuck went with this lady. She took them into her small cottage. In the back room she had what she called her "holy" corner. It was a table in the corner of the room, with a couple of small icons on it and some candles. Up higher in the corner there hung an icon, about the size of a square windowpane. She stood on a chair and took the icon off the wall. When she turned it over, a picture of Lenin was on the back. She had been a schoolteacher for forty years in the big city. This picture of Lenin had hung in her class the entire time. No one knew that behind Lenin's picture was an icon. She said that now Lenin was the one in the corner. This precious lady said that she had come to this village to retire. There she lived with her husband, grown son, and another family member, who were all alcoholics. Now she had to care for all of them, and it was a hard life. She looked at Chuck and began to cry. Then she asked if Chuck thought she was doing right. She wanted his approval for some reason. Again, he put his arm around her and told her that she was doing just right and that God was pleased with her. Remembering the moment, Chuck said, "I am not sure that I have ever met a more faithful follower of God in the midst of such pain and suffering."

They left that cottage and walked to the center of the village. The YIM team was finishing up and getting their things together. It was time to get back on the boat. As the boat pulled away, most of the people from the village were standing on the shore waving at the group. There in the midst of the small crowd of people was that little indigenous woman Chuck had prayed with. She was waving. Her cheeks were still wet with tears, and if Chuck was not mistaken, she was still saying, "Thank you, Jesus." The lesson Chuck and the team learned that day was that God is in control. When you start something new, it is with much prayer and faith in God who will lead you. We have found that he always does. That first village will never be forgotten. It was now up to the Baptist brothers to follow up. It appeared that they were off to a good start. Thank you, Father!

It would be an eight-hour trip to the next village. The team settled in, ate some supper, took in the sights, and turned in for the night. It had been a long day already, and the hard beds down below actually felt good. A few hours into Chuck's rather restful sleep, he was awakened by our volunteer. He was sitting on his bed, and he was short of breath. Chuck asked him what was wrong, and he said that he was having an asthma attack. Chuck asked the man what he could do for him, and the man said that he would just try to go back to sleep. Not much later he woke Chuck up again, and now he was really in trouble. He could hardly catch his breath, and it looked as though his lips were turning blue. He was holding an EpiPen in his hand but seemed frozen, unable to give himself the jab. Without thinking too much about it, Chuck grabbed the pen, stuck it in the man's leg, and held it there for about ten seconds. In a few minutes the man lay back down and seemed to relax.

Chuck went up on deck to tell the captain that there was a problem. It was about three in the morning, and as he went out on the deck, it was as bright as day. We forget that in July it never gets dark in Siberia. It was amazing. The captain decided to divert the boat to a closer village that had a doctor. It took about an hour to get there. They found the village doctor and woke her up. She came to the boat and gave our volunteer a shot of something that helped him. Then a difficult decision had to be made. It was best to turn the boat around and head back to Salekhard, where there would be better medical assistance.

There were no planes available to return to Moscow, so the team stayed in Salekhard for the remainder of their visit. Every day they had reindeer meat for breakfast, lunch, and dinner! There was no water in the hotel, and they had to visit the local bathhouse to bathe. They wrapped their heads in sweatshirts to keep the mosquitoes from biting them badly. Chuck had a kidney-stone attack and was found passed out on the floor of the hotel. There was no communication back to Moscow until finally I received a telegram. Chuck and half the team would be coming home on a certain day, and the remainder the day after.

When Chuck came home from the airport, he didn't look altogether well. He had a wound on his ear and seemed tired and weary. I knew nothing about his kidney stone, nor the fact that he had passed out from the pain, hitting his head on something in the hotel hallway. I didn't know about the volunteer and the asthma attack. In casual conversation once, the volunteer had told me that he had asthma as a child but that he had not had any problem with it for over ten years. I had tucked an EpiPen into his backpack, just in case. Had he not had it, he just might have died. Then Chuck and I thought about Ralph and Mabel Earle, seeing us off at the Kansas City airport and praying protection over us and the ministry every day. What would we have done without the faithful prayers of people like them? We truly are in this together.

SEVEN

Square One

FRANKLIN

IT WAS A BITINGLY COLD, overcast, gloomy day. Late fall weather in Russia is often that way, a precursor to long, dark winters. I was at the "dacha," located a few miles south of Moscow.

Dachas are considered holiday homes, usually only occupied for a part of the year. The dacha tradition in Russia and Ukraine began centuries ago under the rule of the czars, who would give as a gift a small plot of land with a cottage or dwelling to favored and loyal persons. Often those so favored would grow vegetables, enjoy the fresh air, or vacation. The dacha I was at was special. It had been purchased with gifts from Nazarene Youth International, led at the time by Fred Fullerton, as a denominational project. The building was a large two-story structure with enough space for several guests to stay and a large open area. It was ideal for retreats, training sessions, and youth activities.

I was there for a meeting with pastors and missionaries, both Russian and non-Russian. One evening, the scheduled speaker was Chuck Sunberg, the field leader for work in the Commonwealth of Independent States (CIS; the new alliance of nations previously part of the Soviet empire). Getting together in these meetings was important for building relationships and teamwork and for gaining inspiration and information. There were training sessions on ministerial education, compassionate ministries, theology, discipleship, and an amazing variety of other topics required in building a church from scratch. But this night was Chuck's.

After some joyous and enthusiastic choruses in the Russian language and prayer, Chuck stood to speak. I noticed the group of about fifty began to look with anticipation but also with a bemused countenance—they already knew what Chuck was going to say and looked forward to hearing it once again. I wondered what was going on! The rapport he had with the group was obvious, and his sense of humor always appreciated.

As Chuck launched into his speech, I watched a few who were mouthing the words they were hearing. The general outline of the speech was simple, but the content profound. Here is where we came from, how we got here, why we are here, what we believe, how we fit in the larger context of the historic church, where we are going, and, most importantly, where we plan to stay. Chuck would throw in a few Russian words or phrases (these were the early days of language learning) and include anecdotes and humor. As we went along, I began to catch on. This speech was laying the foundation for the church and its leaders.

After the service, I asked some of the Russians about Chuck's presentation. Without exception they laughed and said happily, "Oh, we have heard it before, but we like hearing it again and again. We call it our Square One speech." They added that the next time they met, they knew they would be hearing it again. Only the jokes and anecdotes would change.

Then it dawned on me. Chuck had found the secret for dealing with the core of who we were and instilling that core into the DNA of the new Russian Church of the Nazarene (or Ukrainian Church of the Nazarene or any of the other emerging national churches).

On the last evening of the three-day retreat, we had "fun night." This included games, skits, music, and a lot of conversation. The featured skit was a reenactment of Chuck's Square One speech. These new Nazarenes had it down almost word for word and did not mind throwing a few friendly barbs Chuck's way.

The Eurasia Region in these years was largely a developing region, though it had some of the oldest churches in the denomination (India, the United Kingdom, the Middle East, for example). But there were so many new countries, and many faced the same issue of establishing an identity, a belief structure, a church culture, and protocols. This is not an easy task when there is no precedent or history. Everyone needed a Square One speech. As regional director, I began to talk about the need for Square One, and before long it became a sort of mantra on the Eurasia Region that helped hold us together and give us a common identity.

That dacha became over time a place where people from many places could gather, a kind of grounding place. And Chuck's

Square One speech became a hallmark in the early days of the opening work in the former Soviet Union. Thank you, Chuck Sunberg.

Some Days It Was a Circus

CARLA

Chuck was good about continually reminding the whole team about the mission and focusing on Square One. In reality, it was sometimes hard to keep the mission front and center. There were distractions, some good and some bad. Sometimes, it just felt as if we were in the middle of a three-ring circus.

Once word got out that the Church of the Nazarene would be moving into Russia, Work and Witness teams lined up for the opportunity to come and share in the ministry. There was no official Nazarene work, and yet four teams were on their way to Moscow. Pasadena First Church led the way with Warren Rood, an extraordinary team leader bringing two groups in the first couple of months. They were to partner with the Baptist Union in helping the Baptists build their headquarters, since, as observed earlier, the Baptists were the official sponsors of the Church of the Nazarene in Russia. Day by day, the groups worked, and in the evenings and on weekends, they had the opportunity to tour the city and see the sights that many had only read about during the years of the Cold War.

Trips to Red Square were always a highlight. It was where a person could see the red brick walls of the Kremlin and Saint Basil's Cathedral. A little lesser known, but equally famous, site was that of the Moscow Circus, which, by now, had two locations within the city. Both the old (or Nikulin) and the new (or Bolshoi) circuses had permanent homes in the city of Moscow, and the skills of the performers, animals, and clowns were well known across the Soviet Union. Moscow had the only circus school in the world, where three thousand young students would apply every year for the ninety positions that were available. Of those, only two-thirds would ever find their way to graduation, with a handful being selected for the Moscow circuses and the rest sent to other circuses across the Soviet Union. All said, there is nothing quite like the Moscow Circus, and nearly every team that visited that first summer spent an evening at this extraordinary attraction. Our little girls came to love the opportunity to accompany the teams and soon fell in love with their favorite acts, especially the clown Sergei Prosvirin, whose ability to play the drums and tap-dance had them mesmerized, no matter how many times they attended.

Two vitally important words to our vocabulary were "church" and "circus." The church was important because that was where we worked, where we invited people to attend, and where we hoped people would come to know Christ. The circus was important because it was the place that every out-of-town visitor wanted to go. Often, we took the visitors to the circus on Saturday and invited new people to the church on Sunday. We worked hard at learning those two words: *tserkov* for "church" and *tsirk* for "circus." However, there were times when we, as a family, confused these two words, whether speaking in Russian or in English.

During the first year we were in Moscow, Billy Graham brought his crusade to town. It was a huge event, and thousands of people came from the Russian countryside to attend this crusade, which was titled "Rebirth." The Billy Graham team had worked for months to prepare for the crusade and had asked all the Christian church leaders to partner with them in the project. The major problem they discovered was that there were very few—less than two dozen—churches to invite people to following the event. Christianity had been radically suppressed during the years of Communism, and there had not yet been time to recover. The Union of Evangelical Christians-Baptists led the way and invited the rest of us to support the crusade.

Chuck and I took turns between going to the crusade and staying home with the children. One Sunday, Chuck was preparing to go to the service. It had already been a long day for the girls, and they often longed to get out of our eighth-floor apartment. Our oldest daughter, Christy, then five, pleaded with her father. "Please, take me with you." Her eyes were fixed on her dad, hoping very badly that she could go. At that moment, her little sister, Cara, also chimed in, "Daddy, please, let me go with you." Cara began to sob uncontrollably, "Please, Daddy, please." Chuck and I looked at each other and couldn't understand the attraction of a Billy Graham crusade on a five- and three-year-old. We decided that Christy could go with her dad but that Cara would have to stay home. As Dad and Big Sister went out the door, Cara threw herself on her bed, crying mad. Why did she have to be left behind?

The trip to the crusade started out normal enough, a seven-minute walk between the apartment buildings to the entrance of the metro, or subway. Along the way, the sidewalks around the subway were lined with people selling anything from a loaf of bread or a few cigarettes to even the family china. Everyone was becoming an entrepreneur to survive. Metro Universitet, our local station, was not crowded. The unfriendly escalator monitor was in her usual position, sitting in her glassed-in cage at the bottom of the five-story escalator. She had a sign on her door with the message "I don't give out information." The cleaning ladies were working hard, keeping the station neat and tidy. The floor was speckled with wet sawdust, and the ladies were working this with a broom so that the aging granite floors would look as nice as possible. The wait for the next train was only three minutes.

Soon the dark-blue and turquoise train car, designed in the 1950s, arrived. Once the Communists arrived at a functional plan, they would stick with it. Hence, the circa 1950 train cars and the Lada car, fashioned after the 1960 Fiat. Boarding the train itself was somewhat like stepping into a time capsule. Brown vinyl benches lined the outer walls of the train, and a special section was reserved for the handicapped, the elderly, and those with children. On Sunday afternoons, the train cars were not full and it was easy to find a comfortable place to sit down.

It would take nearly an hour to get to the Olympic stadium, where the crusade would be held. Each stop brought them nearer and nearer to the stadium, but it also brought more and more people into the car. At each stop, people would have to readjust their positions, grabbing a new place on the bar to keep their balance or juggling their bags from one hand to another. Would another stop bring even more people? By now people were pressed up against one another, heads raised to catch their breath. The doors opened, and another rush of people pushed their way into the car. Christy was now on her daddy's lap as he held on to her, trying to keep her from being crushed by the crowd. Finally came the announcement "Next stop, Prospekt Mira."

Because of the crowd, they could not see what awaited them on the platform. Too many people had filled the train station, and yet trainload after trainload of people kept arriving, and the doors kept opening. Chuck tried to keep a tight grip on Christy's hand, but she was so small, down there at the bottom of the crowd. He picked her up and placed her on his shoulders. The situation was frightening, people were packed together so tightly that they moved as one unit, one small movement with your left hip, then with your right, as slow progress was made toward the escalators ahead. Chuck tried to make it fun for Christy, asking her to be his guide. At times it felt as if his feet were no longer touching the ground and that he was simply being swept away by the masses. Eventually, the escalator could be seen up ahead. People were being popped out of the crowd, almost like Ping-Pong balls, and they would land on the first step of the escalator, where they were lifted up and out of the station to safety and the fresh air above.

That day the Russian Red Army Choir sang the "Battle Hymn of the Republic." It's one of those events that remains etched in your memory because, being a child of the Cold War, this was never going to happen. But it did happen. God had broken through the walls, Billy Graham was in Moscow, and the Red Army Choir was singing that their "eyes had seen the glory of the coming of the Lord!" It was a time for "rebirth," and when the altar call was given, thousands went forward not only to learn more about Christ but also to get their hands on the literature that was being distributed. The crowd from the subway station was now the mob heading toward the front of the stadium. The Salvation Army stood guard, trying to keep the people under control, but there were just too many of them. Those trying to disciple or pray with people who had come forward had to throw their literature into the air and run for their lives as they were being crushed. Chuck, seeing his opportunity for departure, headed for the exit, protecting his little girl along the way.

The ride home was rather uneventful, having left before much of the crowd. Finally, arriving back at our metro station, Christy and her daddy made their way in the dark between the big apartment buildings and eventually arrived at home. Christy, normally quite talkative, had been quiet the entire trip home. Maybe she was just tired from the adventure. Taking the elevator to the eighth floor, they exited and then opened the steel door to our apartment. Cara, who had recovered from her tears about five minutes after they had left, bounded to the door to get the full report from her sister. Her daddy and I overheard as Christy finally spoke. She walked into the bedroom with her sister, and letting out a sigh, she said, "It was a service, not the circus!" Cara's eyes brightened as she realized that in her economy, she had gotten the better deal. Raising a little fist in the air, she responded, "Yesss!"

A few months later a professor, Dr. Jonathan Salgado, arrived to teach one of our very first pastoral training courses. Every day, Chuck and Jonathan would have to travel across town, from our apartment to the classroom. Gypsy taxis were the usual mode of transportation. A gypsy taxi was obtained by standing on the curb of a busy street and holding your arm out to your right side. Within a few minutes, a car would usually stop and the negotiations would begin. First, there was the discussion of the destination. If it was out of the way of the driver, he or she would simply drive off without any further conversation. If the driver felt that it was on the way, and it might be advantageous to accept riders, the discussion of payment would begin. The driver would always start with an unrealistically high price. The rider would always say no and then offer an unrealistically low price. The driver would act insulted. The rider would then stand up and act disinterested in the car and behave as though he or she is ready to wave down another. The driver would then lean over and present a price somewhere in the middle. All parties would be happy with this, and the rider would then get into the car to go to his or her destination.

One evening, on their way to class, Chuck and Jonathan were standing on the side of the road, with Chuck's right arm outstretched. A car with Belarusian plates pulled over. Chuck and the driver agreed on a price. As the car headed toward their destination, Chuck decided to practice his Russian skills on the driver. In his broken Russian he asked, "What brings you to Moscow?" The man responded that he was in Moscow working for the *tsirk*, or circus, but Chuck mistook the work for *tserkov* and immediately assumed the man was there on a mission for the Lord. Chuck continued to use the word *tsirk*, thinking he was talking about the church. Chuck was now excited, and he looked at the man and said, "So do I." The driver said, "I don't think so. I've never seen you there." Chuck said, "Maybe that's because I go to a different one." The man said, "Well, there are only two in town, and I know everyone that works there." Chuck wanted to assure the man that good things were happening and that new churches were being planted. He said, "Oh no, now we have many more!" Knowing that there were just two Baptist churches in town, Chuck asked, "Are you a Baptist?" The man looked at him as if he were crazy and responded, "No, I work with horses!" Now Chuck was quite surprised, and he asked him, "You work with horses—in the *tsirk* (circus)?" Chuck was wondering what kind of ministry that might be, still thinking that he was saying *tserkov* (church). The man just looked at him oddly and responded, "Yes, of course, I do." By now the driver was noticeably confused. So was Chuck. Arriving at their destination, Chuck closed the door to the car and finally realized that the driver was talking about the circus!

The lesson we learned was that you had to listen very carefully to catch what people were saying. We didn't know the language very well, so we had to listen to every root form of a word that we would hear, hanging on to the hope that we were catching what was being said. Often, we had to interpret body language as well as verbal language to catch the meaning. Communication had become very hard work! But in the long run, it would be worth it. Eventually, the day would come when we could sit face-to-face with our Russian friends and have heart-to-heart conversations.

Sometimes it felt as though we had to put up with the circus to enable us to get to the church. At least figuratively! Years had to be spent in language study because it's not until you know a people's language that you can truly come to know their heart. People often ask me what I miss about Russia. What I miss is the fellowship. I miss sitting around a small table squeezed into a corner of a crowded kitchen, elbow-to-elbow and face-to-face with my friends, sipping a cup of hot tea. Here is where we really got to know each other, not just on the surface, but heart-to-heart, sharing our burdens and our joys, learning and growing in the Lord.

EIGHT

Nuts and Bolts

FRANKLIN

SO HOW DO YOU OPEN WORK in a vast area of the world to which you have never been and about which you know little? To say the task is daunting, perilous, and overwhelming is an understatement!

Some things are open and obvious, and they mostly revolve around the people who are directly involved—the "boots on the ground." This in-person work encompasses several things: meeting people, conversions, conversations, language, learning the history and culture of the people, and so forth.

But underneath that, mostly out of sight, is what I often think of as the "nuts and bolts." Some call it "laying the foundation." Others call it "instilling the DNA." Whatever you call it, planting for permanence requires some basic things that are not so obvious to the casual observer.

When the Soviet Union (and Eastern Europe) suddenly and dramatically opened under the terms of "perestroika and glasnost," no one had a plan. It had been unforeseen and was, in essence, shock therapy for the organizational structure of the denomination.

I had come to the position of regional director from an eight-year stint in Arizona working with a high-powered group of entrepreneurs who were committed to investing in the kingdom through church planting. They had envisioned acquiring real estate as an investment that could be turned into church sites for new, growing congregations in a high-growth part of the United States.

In my assignment as administrator of that job, I learned that to achieve our objectives with a sense of order, we needed a definitive strategic plan. So I had engaged in this exercise in the three urban areas of the Arizona District: Phoenix and its environs, Tucson, and Las Vegas in Nevada. All were "boom cities" growing rapidly with unlimited possibilities but rapidly escalating prices. Now, here I was living in Europe and facing one of the biggest challenges in the history of missions in the Church of the Nazarene. What to do?

I had heard about and had met Dr. Russ Bredholt several times. A graduate of Olivet Nazarene University, Dr. Bredholt had served as a management and strategic consultant to several high-profile clients across the country. The head of Nazarene Radio and Publications, Dr. Ray Hendrix, had engaged his services in Hong Kong to help create a strategic plan and in the United Kingdom to assist with a communication strategy involving media.

In the meantime, the excitement of opening the work in Russia and elsewhere had infected a number of people who rushed to help, forming up teams to go and see this new opportunity. Some local churches, several colleges, and, in some cases, individuals rushed to secure now-available visas to what had been closed areas. The Sunbergs, having recently arrived to begin the work, found themselves trying to manage these hundreds of visitors, and it was consuming a large amount of their time and energy (let alone finding a place to live and work for themselves, not to mention securing food, as described elsewhere in this book).

One day, Chuck Sunberg saw me at a meeting, and in his forthright style began the conversation with the words "We need $5 million" to acquire some ministry centers across Russia and the Ukraine. He knew, and I knew, and he knew that I knew, that we did not have $5 million or anything even close to that amount available. But for me it was a wake-up call that we better get our act together, develop a plan, and start a process of developing resources.

At some point, I met or called Russ Bredholt and asked him if he would make a trip to Moscow to meet with the Sunbergs and the team and help pull together a plan that everyone could agree on. He agreed, and off he went in the month of January 1993 (the worst possible month to visit frigid Moscow) for several days of meetings. Russ had traveled from Orlando, Florida, to Moscow, wearing a windbreaker that would have been appropriate for Florida in the winter. Unfortunately, it didn't prepare him for the freezing temperatures and biting wind. The Sunbergs were bundled up with their heavy winter coats, layers of socks, hats, and gloves. They took Russ to see Red Square, where he became numb with the cold. Finding a new fast-food restaurant, they stopped for lunch, where Russ tried to warm his hands over the french fries. All of this was preparing him for the days ahead in which he would learn much more about life in the former Soviet Union.

The mission team gathered together—Russians, Ukrainians, Americans, and South Koreans. It was time to examine seriously the overwhelming work that faced them and determine a way forward. There had to be a focus for their efforts that would be foundational for what could be built in the years ahead. I had told Chuck and Carla about the work in Cuba, where the missionaries had not prepared the local ministers for leadership. When the revolution came, the missionaries had to evacuate in a rush, leaving a denominational manual and keys to the property on the kitchen table. I challenged the Sunbergs to imagine that they only had ten years to establish the work and that the doors just might close. What would they do in those ten years? That became the foundation for the conversation with Russ and what would become the strategic plan.

In Russ's own words, "Once the meetings concluded with the Sunberg team, Chuck came to my room (in a formerly Communist meeting center), where we took the Strategic Mission Plan outline and filled in [the blanks]." One of the interesting points of discussion was on "hopeless opportunities." Lonnie and Connie Norris, working in Volgograd, Russia, spent time describing the hopelessness that they had discovered in the Volgograd region. It was this hopelessness that provided unending opportunities for ministry. Needs that were not being met became a part of the strategic plan.

While the team on the field was developing a strategic plan, Chuck had planned to meet with several business executives who had an interest in what the Lord was doing in the former

Soviet Union. Early on we had watched as other Christian organizations had challenged people, including Nazarenes, to become donors to this new frontier. We watched as literally hundreds of thousands of dollars, or maybe even millions, were given to parachurch organizations by our wonderful and caring Nazarenes. At the same time, the challenge was as big, or even bigger, for a mission that would result in church planting. This was a long-term investment that would sow seeds toward something permanent.

Chuck reached out to Dr. Louie Bustle, who was now the head of World Mission. He told him about the need for funding, the strategic plan, and the vision of reaching the former Soviet Union. Finally, Dr. Bustle told him, "You can spend all that you can raise." From this came the need to form a partnership of people who could invest money in opening the work. Mr. Merritt Mann, another full-time volunteer and longtime executive with IBM out of Washington, DC, helped form what would eventually become the CIS Partnership. In one of the first meetings in Indianapolis during the 1993 General Assembly, one of the business executives asked if there was a strategic plan. Chuck very calmly pulled out of his briefcase "The Strategic Plan," and everyone was duly impressed. Business executives who invest in a project want to see the plan because "return on investment" is very important. And in this case, the return was to be a permanent church that would potentially impact hundreds of people for Christ and the kingdom.

One of the business executives was inspired by the need to train pastors for the next generation of leadership. The executives were looking at the intense, ten-year investment in laying a strong foundation, and this meant training pastors. Jay

Meador from Indianapolis said that he would make an initial investment that would bring together Nazarene educators from around the world to design a program for theological education in the former Soviet Union. This became the seed money for what became affectionately known as the "Kyiv Consultation." By this time, Jon and Kathy Mowry had moved to the field to work on the development of theological education. Bob and Colleen Skinner had moved from the Philippines to Kyiv to lead the work there. The Skinners worked on all the details as the Sunbergs, Mowrys, and others planned to meet with those invited to the "consultation." Dr. Jerry Lambert, Education Commissioner for the Church of the Nazarene, had helped put together the invitations. Dr. Kent Hill, who was now president of Eastern Nazarene College, came along with John Haines, regional education coordinator; Dr. Roger Hahn from Nazarene Theological Seminary; Christian Sarmiento, specialist in distance education from Mesoamerica; and Wes Tracy from headquarters in Kansas City. Others were members of the newly formed partnership, and some had come along on a vision tour.

The "Kyiv Consultation" will go down in history as one of the coldest events held by the Church of the Nazarene. Arriving in October, the guests discovered the Soviet system of central heating. The government had not turned on the heat yet, nor was there hot water in the "hotel" where everyone was staying. As the group gathered in the morning, they would regale one another with tales of their attempts to stay warm. Every blanket was in use. Some were wearing every piece of clothing they had brought with them and were simply changing what was on top each day. Another would warm the bed with a blow-dryer before jumping in at night, wrapping in the thin blankets, and topping it off with the carpet from the floor. In this place, the team hammered out a set of twenty-four modular courses to be used as a curriculum or course of study to train pastors. Once the framework was put together, Kent Hill, John Haines, and the Mowrys stayed up late at night to fill in the details so that by the time the consultation was finished, a product was in hand and a road map charted to move forward.

Dr. Lambert took a copy of that newly updated strategic plan for theological education with him to America. There he happened to make the acquaintance of a woman who was managing the trust of a couple who had been interested in Christian ministry and education around the world. Dr. Lambert pulled out the plan, and the Maslund Trust gave a grant of $400,000 to develop the concept for the Church of the Nazarene in the former Soviet Union.

That grant led to a program in theological education that would become all-encompassing. Not only would it prepare pastors in the field, but it would also raise up a native Russian-speaking faculty who would lead the church well into the future. Partnerships were developed with European Nazarene College, Nazarene Theological Seminary in Kansas City, and Nazarene Theological College in Manchester, England. Professors from around the globe would invest in the students of the former Soviet Union. Some of the very best individuals that the church had to offer gave of themselves and would come and teach, including Tom Noble, Alex Deasley, Fletcher Tink, Joseph Coleson, and Rob Staples. Not only did they teach, but they also invested in the lives of the students, and as a result, seven leaders received master's degrees from Nazarene Theological Seminary and four went on to receive doctor of philosophy degrees from Nazarene Theological College (NTC) and the

University of Manchester. Dr. Svetlana Khobnya, originally from Volgograd, is the senior lecturer in biblical studies and languages, serving the global Church of the Nazarene at NTC.

The need for a plan led to a strategic plan, which led to a seed donation, which developed a full-blown concept, which resulted in major funding. Chuck and the field were well on their way to the $5 million and the development of a foundation that would survive the departure of the missionaries. The partnership began to take shape and, as of this writing, continues to work hand in hand with the field leadership in the former Soviet Union.

NINE

Hopeless Opportunities

CARLA

With God all things are possible.
—Matthew 19:26

Armenia

On December 7, 1988, at 11:41 a.m. local time, an earthquake that registered 6.8 on the Richter scale hit the country of Armenia. The epicenter was about six miles from the town of Spitak, a town of 30,000 inhabitants. Including the surrounding area, at least 25,000 people died that day, with some estimates as high as 50,000. Nearly 130,000 people were injured. As a result, the Soviet Union struggled to respond to the tragedy. The inability of the Soviet Union to adequately respond to the needs of their own people revealed the weakness of the system to the world. It became obvious that the situation was becoming desperate. Winter was upon the people of Armenia, the snow was falling, the temperatures were plummeting, and the people were overwhelmed.

In time, aid began to come in from other parts of the world, including help from the Church of the Nazarene. While we did not have official work in the Soviet Union yet (that would come in 1992), Nazarene Compassionate Ministries (NCM) received permission to build a sewing retraining center near the town of Gyumri, Armenia. Armenians of the diaspora had sent funds through NCM to help minister to those who had been impacted by the earthquake. There were many individuals who found themselves disabled after having suffered crushing injuries. Soviet-era buildings had been erected throughout the republic, and these were not designed to be earthquake proof. The Armenians, having lived in the region since the time of Noah, knew how to build strong buildings, not more than three to five stories tall, that would survive the frequent quakes. The Soviet system reused building plans across the entire nation. If it was good enough for Moscow, it must work in Yerevan, Armenia! Multistory family dwellings were built, sometimes twenty or more stories tall. The old corrupt Soviet system also played a key role. Why put all the materials into the building of a structure, such as the right strength of steel or the correct mix of concrete, when "extra" materials could be sold off to fill the pockets of the manager or supervisor? When the "big one" hit, the results were catastrophic because the Soviet buildings collapsed like a house of cards. This is what impacted both the death rate and the types of injuries. The Nazarene sewing center was primarily established to retrain people who had lost their legs into a new profession. The center was started shortly after the 1988 earthquake.

When we arrived in Moscow in June 1992, one of our assignments was to travel to Armenia and check on the center. In December of that year, Roy Campbell, Tanya Arakcheeva, and Chuck were to fly to Yerevan and to visit the sewing center. When they arrived at the airport in Moscow, Tanya went up to the counter to check on the flight. She returned to tell Chuck and Roy that their flight had been canceled and would not be leaving until the following day. Chuck asked Tanya to ask the lady at the counter about any other flights that might be going to Armenia. Tanya returned and said that there was a plane going to Armenia at the same time as their flight was supposed to go. Chuck asked why the lady hadn't told them about that flight, and the response was that they had not asked about that one, but about today's flight. The flight leaving today was yesterday's flight, which was delayed until today, so today's flight would be leaving tomorrow. They asked if there were three seats on yesterday's flight, and sure enough, yes, there were. When they asked why she did not tell them that to begin with, she said it was because they had asked about today's flight, and it was leaving tomorrow. Then, they asked if they could get tickets on yesterday's flight that was going today. She said that they could. Again, they asked why she didn't give them that information earlier. She gave the same response as before, that they had only asked about today's flight, not yesterday's. After all that, they found themselves flying on yesterday's flight that was scheduled to arrive today because today's flight would not arrive until tomorrow. However, the flight was delayed, so they arrived tomorrow on yesterday's flight that didn't leave until today. Beyond that, who knows. Four hours later they landed safe and sound, but a little confused.

Again, this was during a time when borders were rapidly changing as everyone was adjusting to the new reality of no longer being the Soviet Union. Because countries were now independent, new permissions were required to enter them and, in turn, new permission was required to again enter Russia. Six months earlier, none of this would have been necessary. Roy Campbell had a Soviet-era visa, and once he left Russia, he did not have any visa entries to return to Russia. This was not discovered until the moment the three of them were getting ready to board the plane. (And a lot had happened to just get them on the plane.) After a few moments of debate, the three decided to board the plane in Moscow for the Armenian capital of Yerevan, not knowing how they were going to get Roy back into Russia after the trip.

When they arrived in Yerevan, the situation was dire. Armenia was at war with the neighboring country of Azerbaijan. All resources were invested in the war effort, and it left little for the folks at home. It was very cold at the time, and they only had electricity for one hour a day, if even that. The three of them were to be there for four days, and during that entire time, they did not take off one stitch of clothing. Boy, was it cold!

The first day they set out on the four-hour drive from Yerevan to Gyumri. As they were driving along, the driver pointed to the vast field to right. He said, "That used to be a forest." It was barren land as far as you could see. The people had cut it all down to keep warm. Amazing!

The road was filled with large potholes. It was slow going on both sides of the road, but eventually they arrived, and what they saw was shocking. Most of the buildings were uninhabitable because of the earthquake. The people had taken the shipping containers that had been brought in the international aid and turned them into houses. They were to be guests in one of those containers for dinner that evening. Chuck was surprised at how nice it was inside, although it was so cold outside that there was frost halfway up the sides of the container walls. It was interesting how resourceful the people had become after such devastation.

They visited the sewing center and heard how thankful the people were for the help. It made them proud of our church because it had helped these people in their hour of need. Nazarene Compassionate Ministries does good work all over the world. Like Armenia, everywhere there are hopeless opportunities to which we might be willing to open our eyes and become the hands and feet of Jesus.

The team made their way back to Yerevan for the night. In the morning, their thoughts turned to Roy Campbell. How would they get him back into Russia? They fully expected the Russian border guards to turn him away and send him back to Armenia. They headed to the airport, talked their way onto the plane, and took off for Moscow. The three of them were also praying off and on the whole flight. Could the Lord help Roy get back into Moscow? After flying for a while, the plane started to descend. What was unusual was that they had not flown long enough to make it to Moscow. They could see through the window of the plane that it was very cloudy outside. They continued descending but did not break through the clouds. They did not see the ground until they were about to land, only a few hundred feet in the air. As they were taxiing in, Tanya looked out the window and said, "This is not Moscow." Chuck told her that it had to be. She said again, "This is not Moscow."

The plane came to a halt, stairs were wheeled up to the door, and an official entered. She told them that they had landed six hundred kilometers east of Moscow because the capital was blanketed with thick fog. The lady said that there were three options: first, wait in the terminal for the fog to lift in Moscow, which could be a few days; second, take the train; or third, take the fourteen-hour bus ride to Moscow. They got off the plane and gathered their bags. Tanya checked on the train, but there were no seats available. She checked the bus and purchased the last three tickets for this motley crew just trying to get home.

The fourteen-hour bus trip was crowded and bumpy. It was also very cold, but Chuck's seat was right by the heater that continually belched out hot air. He was very warm, maybe too warm, still in all the clothing he had worn for days. After traveling all night, in the light of the dawn, the bus pulled up to a subway stop in Moscow. It was just a regular subway stop, with kiosks selling what little they had, people heading to work, and the regular hustle and bustle of life. As the three exited the bus, there were no border guards, no one asking for papers, no long lines, just the entrance to the subway. The three of them reached the subway and then went their separate ways.

The following day, the team gathered in our little office in Moscow as we heard about their interesting journey. Chuck mentioned that he had prayed that God would blind the border guards when Roy went through. Tanya said, "I prayed that God would close all the airports in Moscow." There happen to be five airports surrounding the city, and God closed them all. Tanya's faith was inspiring. God closed Moscow for us. The next day in the paper, there was an article about the thick fog in Moscow. The article said that this was the first time anything like that had ever happened and that all the airports were closed at the same time. Hopeless opportunities! Shaking his head, Chuck said out loud, "With God all things are possible!" Tanya went on to attend European Nazarene College and returned to pastor Moscow First Church of the Nazarene. Today, she and her husband are serving as missionaries.

Ulyanovsk

Testifying to the work of God is vitally important. Telling people around the global church about how God is working is necessary to build up our own faith, as well as that of others. The Church of the Nazarene is an interconnected global family, filled with brothers and sisters who help one another out. That is the beauty of this global church.

While traveling, whether in other parts of the region or to the United States, we wanted the faithful members of the church to know the story of Nazarene missions. On home assignment, Chuck and I would go in different directions to tell the story, because there was so much interest in what was happening in the former Soviet Union. We did our best each time we came home to cover as much territory as possible.

On one trip to the United States, Chuck was speaking at a district missions convention. After he had spoken in the morning, a Nazarene farmer came up to him with tears in his eyes. He said that he wanted to help us. Chuck thanked him and asked what that meant. He said that he wanted to give us the proceeds from his best producing field each year. He could not tell us exactly how much that would be because things change, but he promised to send what he received each year. They prayed together, Chuck thanked him again, and then Chuck continued his journey to the next stop to resume telling the story. That is just one example of how faithful our people are. In many cases, they give generously, over and above their tithe. It has been a privilege to meet our wonderful, God-loving, missions-loving people.

It was our constant prayer to ask God where he wanted us to plant the next church. When you start from nothing, your ears tend to be especially tuned to God's voice and his leading. It always amazed us how faithful God was to answer our prayers. One day, we received a phone call from a lady we had never met. Her name was Masha, and she was from the town of Ulyanovsk, a city about six hundred miles east of Moscow. We asked her how she got our number, and then she began to tell us her story. She told us that she had been a good Communist and an atheist. Some months before, she became very ill and had to be hospitalized. Nothing could be done for her, and the doctors told her that she was going to die. One night as she was lying in her hospital room, she cried out to God. "If you are really there, please help me and I will follow you." A little while later, she said, an angel walked into her room and touched her. The angel told her that she would get better and that she needed to be faithful to God.

A friend of Masha's had met an American gentleman and had moved with him to Oklahoma. One day while they were communicating, Masha told her friend about what had happened to her. While in Oklahoma, her friend had begun attending a church called the Church of the Nazarene. Her friend encouraged Masha to find that church in Russia. It took her some time, and a bit of searching, but finally, she found our number and called. She invited us to come to her town to help her start a church.

We didn't know anything about the town of Ulyanovsk. It had not been our plan to go way out there to plant a church, but it was God's plan. In the meantime, we tried to help Masha through phone calls, encouraging her to seek God with all her heart. We also invited her to all the meetings we had with our pastors on the field. She was like a dry sponge, soaking in everything that she could about Christ and the church.

We were finally able to visit Masha in her hometown. Interestingly, this was the hometown of Vladimir Ilyich Lenin, whose real last name was Ulyanov. Lenin was simply a code name taken during the time of the revolution. This city proudly bore his name and was the destination of many a pilgrim wanting to connect to "Father Lenin." There were museums throughout the town, with plaques marking where he lived as a child and in later years. The airport was cavernous, with the runway created for the thousands of faithful who would arrive by plane, visiting this historic city year after year. It was home to the UAZ (Ulyanovsky Avtomobilny Zavod) car factory, where jeep-like, off-road vehicles were produced. They had been vital to the nation during the war effort. But now, when we arrived, it was something different. One small plane, a Yak-40, arrived each day. This was a plane with a turbofan jet engine and was one of the first Soviet-era planes to be deemed airworthy by Western countries. While it looked like little more than a bus with wings, it had proven to be a mighty staple in the Aeroflot (Russian airline) system. However, it is miniscule in size compared to the larger Ilyushins and Tupolevs that landed by the hour during the glory days of the Ulyanovsk airport, which boasts the third longest runway in the world.

It was winter when we arrived, and the airport was staffing a skeleton crew. The tarmac was covered in snow, and yet we were able to land. A path had been carved in the snow from the plane to the terminal. After exiting the plane, we followed an airline staff member single file through the little path in the snow. The lights weren't on in the terminal, it was dark and musty, and it was clearly a shadow of its earlier days. We were hustled to a small room that had no heat, and there we waited until a cart arrived with the luggage.

We were greeted by Masha and her family. It was such a warm welcome, and we were overwhelmed by their hospitality. She had gathered a growing group of people who were interested in learning all they could about the Lord and the Bible. We met with them on a Sunday morning in a small office, where they assembled each week because no one would rent this new "sect" a place to meet. It was crowded. They told us that this was only about half the group because they had to alternate coming to church. Half would come one week, and the other half would come the next. Interestingly, in the office, on top of a tall cabinet, was a large bust of Lenin. They had Chuck speak standing by that cabinet with Lenin looking over his shoulder. It was all so surreal.

Meeting this group of all-new believers was a real joy. They were anxious to learn, and they were so excited about their newfound faith. What a blessing! Before we left, they asked us about how to go about getting a permanent place to meet. We told them that we would help them all we could, but that it was up to them to look around and figure it out. The last thing we told them was that we had $10,000 designated for them when the time came to find a meeting place. They were grateful for the visit and the promise of help.

Several weeks later we received a call from Masha's son. He had already become a vital leader in the group, partnering with his mother. He was so excited. He told us that they had found a piece of land with a small, run-down building to turn into a church, and it was on the main street in town. We asked him the name of that street, and he proudly told us: "Karl Marx Boulevard." Chuck's mind was already wandering, thinking about a church named Karl Marx Boulevard First Church of the Nazarene. You can't make this stuff up.

We asked him how much they needed. He said it could be bought for $21,000. We told him that we only had $10,000. He said that he knew that and reminded us that it was on the main street. He said they needed to give the owners an answer by ten the next morning. We told him that we were sorry but that, again, all we had was $10,000. He was disappointed but understood.

Chuck and I had a morning routine. We would get up, eat breakfast, get the girls off to school, have devotions, and then check our email for what had come while we were asleep. America was awake while we slept, and there was always a full inbox in the morning! There in Chuck's morning mail was a note from that faithful Nazarene farmer. He wanted us to know that he had sent a check from the sale of the crop from his best field. He apologized for not telling us sooner, but it was a check for $11,000. He hoped that we could find a place to put it to the best use. We could not wait to call the folks in Ulyanovsk. The phone rang and rang. We were about to hang up when someone answered. It was the son. He sounded very tired. I asked him what was wrong, and he said they had stayed up all night long praying for God to help them with this purchase. Then Chuck told him about receiving the email and that they could buy the land. God had provided the additional money during the night! He dropped the phone, and we could hear voices praising the Lord and shouting. Then he got back on the phone and said, "You are right, Pastor Chuck! It is true! With God all things are possible!"

In the process of fashioning Ulyanovsk as the Communist center through the years, Communist officials had destroyed most of the churches in the region. So, when the leaders of the city heard that a new religious sect had purchased property on Karl Marx Boulevard, they may have said to themselves, "Over Lenin's dead body!" The miracle was that they decided to trade us the property in the middle of town for an unfinished building in the middle of an apartment complex. The new site they traded to us was much better for people to access and was in the middle of a neighborhood of people who needed to know Christ. We have sent Work and Witness teams there over the years, and now it is a nice place for a thriving group of believers to meet, and they can all come every Sunday. Did we mention that this was in Lenin's hometown? And that this wasn't a part of our strategic plan? Evidently, it's true that "with God all things are possible."

TEN

Initiatives: The Power of Media

FRANKLIN

IN THE SUMMER OF 1944, the general assembly of the Church of the Nazarene, meeting in Minneapolis, passed a resolution creating the Nazarene Radio League. This recognized the power of media in extending the mission and message of the church.

By 1945, a decision was made to create a nationwide radio program. The old 1883 hymn, written by Daniel Whittle, titled "Showers of Blessing" was adopted as both the theme and name of the new program. During the 1940s and 1950s, the radio coverage expanded dramatically. Soon a Spanish equivalent named "La Hora Nazarena" was created to cover the rapidly expanding ministry of the church in Spanish-speaking countries. Over time this was followed by an expansion into several other languages. Millions of people listened to these radio programs.

By 1990, Dr. Ray Hendrix, who had grown up in Argentina, oversaw both literature development in non-English constituencies and what was called "Nazarene Radio." During the Cold War, the idea of creating a Russian broadcast became an important goal. This was done in cooperation with ERF, an evangelistic German media corporation that was already broadcasting in several language areas in the Soviet Union and Eastern Europe.

Providentially, by now Nikolaj Sawatzky and his family had graduated from European Nazarene College and were soon employed to assist with Russian language ministries, including radio. Nikolaj and his wife, Lydia, had been reared in Russia but were of German descent, part of the great migration of Germans to develop the agricultural interest of Russia that was promoted by Catherine the Great, czarina of Russia. They had been able to leave Russia in the mid-1970s, and, in God's own timing, now were highly qualified people both linguistically and spiritually. They were available to carry on pioneering ministries as part of the regional office through literature and radio in the Russian language.

Meantime, ironically, the Soviet government had provided a simple radio without an off button to every family home in Russia. The radio had one channel, thus enabling the government to put into every home their propaganda, information, and policies. With the Soviet system crumbling, these "always on" radios now became instruments that could be used by others, such as the ERF and Nazarene Radio.

Two things, among many, were required for a Russian broadcast: money and music. The financial backing for this enterprise was undertaken by Nazarene Missions International, whose president was the legendary Africa missionary Dr. Louise Robinson Chapman, widow of Dr. J. B. Chapman, general superintendent. She spearheaded the fundraising and through personal interest raised in offerings hundreds of thousands of dollars for the Russian Radio effort.

But what about music? Where could religious music in the Russian language and of high quality be secured? Enter Bryansk and the Russian Baptist church, which had a choir that had made quite a splash with their excellent singing. Dr. Hendrix and others had heard of them and suggested an exploratory visit.

Bryansk is a city near the Ukrainian border that the Soviet government had declared closed. Many of the Soviet army tanks and other munitions were produced in this city of almost half a million people, and foreigners were for many years banned from the city. Nonetheless, five church leaders climbed aboard a train in Moscow for the fourteen-hour trip to Bryansk. The five were regional director Franklin Cook; Ray Hendrix; Randy Beckum from the regional office; Chuck Sunberg, newly appointed missionary; and Nikolaj Sawatzky from the regional office.

Rattling along the tracks, the group hardly knew what to expect. They arrived at a spooky train station in Bryansk at around midnight—it was dark, it was cold, and it was strange. However, the senior pastor from the Russian Baptist church and some of his people met the group with a warm, enthusiastic welcome. They were escorted to a large, two-story, rambling house that predated the Great Patriotic War (World War II). This is where the senior pastor lived. Each was taken to a room with a bed and told to "have a wonderful night." The strange sounds and surroundings kept most of them awake. Franklin Cook was placed in a large central room with no windows but plenty of curtains leading to other rooms. Sometime around five in the morning, he noticed the curtains beginning to move with pairs of eyes staring at him. As it turns out, the pastor had at least ten, and perhaps more, children, and they were more than curious about who these strange foreigners were (remember, foreigners were not allowed).

Then it was breakfast time—the inevitable tea, black bread, and some eggs. And soon, the entire family showed up, and the five visiting leaders were caught up in a swirl of generosity and enthusiasm. That is, until the men, including the five leaders, were escorted to an adjoining porch and told to disrobe. They were about to have a uniquely Russian business meeting.

One member of the group of five said, "Excuse me?" Again, as the Russians were disrobing, they said that group members were to take their clothes off. Evidently, they were going to learn that many business transactions happen in the Russian banya, or sauna. There was a certain protocol to be followed.

Reluctantly, they complied. Once the men were all "unclothed," they were taken into the sauna, which had been warmed up most of the morning. There were three levels of wooden seats, like small bleachers, in the sauna. There weren't quite enough seats for all of them, so some had to sit on the floor. All morning the brothers had stoked the fire to get it real hot to see if the foreigners could handle it. It was indeed hot!

After several minutes, Franklin asked Ray how he was doing. Ray, who was sitting on the floor groaning, replied, "I think I am going to throw up!" It was so hot! Soon the group was invited to leave the sauna and go into the next room, where there was, what appeared to be, a cow trough filled with cool water. All five got in that trough. Oh, did that cool water feel good! After the group was there awhile, the brothers invited them to come back into the room where this entire adventure had started. This was the room with the couches and comfortable chairs. Each was given a towel. They were the size of a tea towel. There they were, fully unclothed, with a little tea towel, sitting around and talking about Russian radio. They were told that was the only way business was officially negotiated, in the banya. That would have been good information to have had before the trip. Probably most of the group would have declined to go.

After they had been talking awhile, one of the Russian hosts asked, "Who is first?" "First for what?" was the brisk response from the group. One by one they were taken back into the hot sauna to be flogged with birch branches. The problem was that the walls were thin, and the rest of the group could hear the groans as the beatings took place. They were told that it had something to do with opening your pores and making you healthy. It was Chuck's plan to go last so that the guy doing the "beating" would be tired. Unfortunately, when it was finally his turn, a new guy showed up. He only had one eye, and that one eye was on Chuck. Chuck followed the brother into the sauna, where he lay down on the bench and braced himself. He gritted his teeth so the others would not hear him grunting in the next room. After he finished "beating" Chuck up and down the backside, the brother said those dreaded words that shook Chuck to the core: "Turn over!" Reluctantly, Chuck did as he was told, and before long the health treatment was complete. By the time Chuck returned to the other room, the negotiations were over and the deal was made. The hosts told them that they like the sauna better in the winter because instead of the cool pool, they go out and roll in the snow. The team never went back to get that experience!

That evening, after an outdoor dinner with members of the church, the group gathered back at the pastor's house and began comparing bruises and wounds from their beatings. When Chuck lifted his shirt, he was fire red on both sides. He has grass allergies, and apparently birch leaves affect him the same way. He got the prize for looking the most scarred.

The time with the brothers was good and successful. Their music was used for our radio programs, but getting the deal done was a once in a lifetime experience. To God be the glory!

ELEVEN

Connecting

CARLA

ONE OF THE GREATEST CHALLENGES of beginning a new work is knowing where to connect. How does one build relationships within a new community and especially one in which the culture and language are new to you?

Dr. Kent Hill, along with his wife, Jan, and their two children, had come to Moscow while serving as the president of the Institute on Religion and Democracy and was teaching at Moscow State University. Kent was a member of the Church of the Nazarene, but he was also an expert on religion in the Soviet Union. His 1991 book *The Soviet Union on the Brink: An Inside Look at Christianity and Glasnost* became must-read material for anyone coming to do mission work in the former Soviet Union. His connections were invaluable, and we were compelled to listen to his guidance.

The Hills had lived in the Bittsa sports complex for months while Kent was giving lectures. Jan had taught English at a local Russian school, located just across the main road from the Bittsa. There, they worked with the school director, Anatoly, who had a penchant for playing jazz on his trumpet, as well as participating in iron-man competitions. Wanting to hand off the baton of their work before they returned to America, Kent worked tirelessly to find us an apartment, as well as to connect us with Anatoly. Soon we, as well as Mark Mann, who had volunteered to return after his time with the Youth in Mission teams, would become English teachers. This provided an incredible opportunity to spend time with Russian young people and learn about their life and culture.

Anatoly and his wife, Svetlana, wanted to help us with our new work. We were already meeting on Sundays with the young people at the Bittsa horse arena, and they came to join us. They also brought along their children. This was a second marriage for both of them, and so their blended family would join us most Sundays for worship. Soon fall was giving way to winter, and we were learning how to adjust to life in what felt like a black-and-white movie with a dim light bulb. Living this far north, the days became extremely short, and we learned to walk our daughter Christy to kindergarten in the moonlight and bring her home in the dark as well. The sun only shone for a few hours in the middle of the day.

Not only was the cold now upon us, but also the food shortages continued. The only green vegetables we could find were pickles in the market (to this day our girls love pickles). The problem wasn't as bad for us as it was for the pensioners. On fixed incomes, and with rampant inflation, they were now getting the equivalent of eight United States dollars a month. Anatoly's wife, Svetlana, came to us and told us about the difficulties in the country. She had a passion for those who were in need. I had been asked to serve as the Nazarene Compassionate Ministries (NCM) coordinator and was just learning what this role might mean. Steve Weber was the head of NCM in Kansas City at the time, and he had come to Moscow to talk to us about ways that NCM might help us in ministering. He had told us that sometimes when you begin a new work, you need to hire a good "cigar-smoking presbyterian" to help you get going. You see, when you begin an entirely new work in a new country that has very few believers, you just might have to hire people to help you who may not yet be quite with you. (A few years later, as the work was being started in Saint Petersburg, our team hired musicians from the circus to help with worship services. Chuck visited one Sunday, and as he stood to lead the people in prayer, the keyboard player plunked out an intro worthy of a circus act.)

Although Svetlana was new to all that we were doing, because of her passion for those in need, we hired her to be our NCM coordinator in Moscow, and she was simply amazing. This was a woman full of creativity and energy to spare. She wrote up a plan to go to the local government minister and ask for a group of pensioners in the community near the Bittsa that needed help with food. We adopted these families, and through the generosity of Nazarenes around the globe, we began providing food every month. Svetlana would go and do all the shopping. She would find enough sugar, cooking oil, tea, dried beans, rice, pasta, eggs, and canned goods to make a well-stocked bag of food to supplement a pensioner for a month. We began regular visits with Svetlana to the homes of these elderly, who often wept when someone showed up to give them food. One day Svetlana, along with Misha, who was working regularly with Roy Campbell, arrived at an apartment to discover that the pensioner had nearly died. The gas was on in the oven, and the pensioner's younger relative had left it on to kill the grandparent so that the relative could inherit the apartment. A life was saved.

Another pensioner who received food was Alexander. He lived a couple of kilometers from where the church was meeting, but he was so overwhelmed by the food that he wanted to come and meet the people at the church. He began coming every week and gave his life to Jesus. He had faithfully served the Communist Party as a guard at the Kremlin, but now, at nearly eighty years of age, he and his wife were childless. Most of their married life they had waited to be given an apartment. While waiting, they slept in the kitchen of an apartment they shared with two other families. Now they had an apartment but were lonely and had little food to survive. One Sunday morning, it was minus forty-five degrees Celsius and the buses were not running because the diesel fuel was too thick at that temperature to function properly. Our little family arrived at the church after getting there in a car that was nearly frozen. As we pulled up for worship, there was Alexander standing outside. His face was red, ice forming on his cheeks, but he was bundled up in a fur coat and hat. We asked how he got there, and he told us that he had walked. Then he said, "After so many years of not knowing Christ, I couldn't miss one Sunday." The one Sunday he didn't show up at church, we discovered he'd gone home to be with Jesus.

Svetlana not only helped us minister to the poor and needy but also had her own connections. I'm not sure we will ever really know the extent of those connections, but she used them to help with the work of the church.

Before we even knew that there would be work in Russia, God had been speaking to faithful Nazarenes. Dr. Nina Gunter was the global director of Nazarene Missions International, and everywhere she went, she inspired people to become a part of the missional enterprise of the church. Whether talking with family or friends, she left people wanting to become a part of something much bigger than themselves. This was the case with a friend of hers from South Carolina who decided to donate $150,000 for a church in Russia—before there was work in Russia! Somewhere along the way, another donor had given $15,000 for a church in Russia as well. As the work began in Moscow, real estate prices were fluctuating. No one really knew the value of anything, since nothing had been held by private individuals in over seventy years. While inflation was rocketing in the country, real estate suddenly became a very hot commodity.

Studying the context into which you have been called to serve is always important. The Russian context, and beyond, was one that was quite foreign to the missionary work of the Church of the Nazarene. Nothing in this place seemed to make sense. The church had always worked with the marginalized, and that usually meant those who had not been exposed to education and good medical care or opportunities for work. In this case, because the literacy rate was close to 100 percent, education wasn't a problem. They found marginalized nuclear scientists who were driving cabs because they suddenly found themselves unemployed and trying to survive. This was such a big problem that the airport had to install Geiger counters just to catch those who might be trying to smuggle in or out nuclear material to make a few dollars. We immersed ourselves in Russian literature, trying to learn everything that we could. We read Tolstoy, Dostoyevsky, and Pushkin. We read the history of the czars and studied all that we could about Russian Orthodoxy. And of course, none of this would make sense without studying the language. Learning to listen and speak is how you discover the heart of a people.

Language study would be one of the most difficult challenges we would face. Because everything had happened so quickly with the fall of the Berlin Wall and all the changes in Eastern Europe, there were no plans for language school. The reality was that the world, not just the church, was unprepared for what happened. There were very few schools that taught Russian to foreigners, either inside or outside the Soviet Union. We hired a language teacher who began with grammar. Russian grammar is extremely complex, and when we asked how long it took Russians to learn, we were told about twelve years—all of their time in school. Chuck and I took our lessons together, which we learned was not a good idea. People learn languages differently and at varying speeds. I already spoke German and English, and as a third-culture kid, I seemed to have some proficiency at learning languages. For Chuck, this was a new venture, and it was extremely difficult. We lasted about two weeks in the same class together and then decided that if our marriage was to survive, we needed to take separate classes. We heard about this experience being repeated in many a family engaged in language study. It would take us years to wrestle with Russian, but with the language came the context and thus the understanding of the heart.

Part of the context was to recognize the value of permanence to the people of the former Soviet Union. To be a church meant to have a building. There has been much discussion about the importance of house churches, and in some contexts that church model will work. Also, it may work if there are enough anchor churches for support. However, in the former Soviet Union, an area that had been so impacted by Russian Orthodoxy, to not have a building was to not be a church. The people of God had to gather, and the liturgy had to be celebrated and chanted for there to be true worship. We understood that for there to be a long-term commitment to the work in the former Soviet Union, buildings or ministry centers would need to be a part of that strategy. These would be locations from where we would engage in the preaching, teaching, and healing ministry of Jesus Christ.

Svetlana helped us search for a building in Moscow. We knew that our rental time would run out at the Bittsa sports complex, and then it would be difficult to find a new home. We visited with the so-called local prince of the district, who was responsible for a population of over two million people, including all public buildings. In principle, all the buildings were public buildings. Even when the apartments were privatized, the government still owned the outside of the buildings and was responsible for their care. All schools, businesses, and offices were owned by the government. No wonder he was the "prince." We contacted the prince because we were hoping that he might have an abandoned building that could be turned into a church. At the time there were several unused buildings in the area, especially old kindergartens, and we were praying that the Lord might provide. Instead of providing, the man laughed at us and said, "I don't have a single church in my district, and I can't imagine why I would need one." He then sent us on our way. I think we all tucked that response away in our minds and pondered it for the future. The idea that there was not a single church in an area of two million people—not even an Orthodox church—was indeed something to consider. At one time, denominational leaders in the Church of the Nazarene in the United States used to encourage planting churches for every fourteen thousand people. Considering the size of the high-rise apartment buildings in the former Soviet Union, you would need a church for nearly every city block! The prince needed 143 churches in his district, and he didn't even have one. We continued to pray.

It was more than a year later when Svetlana, always poring over advertisements in the newspaper, discovered that some businesses were being privatized, which also meant that they would then own their buildings. Often, we would go and peruse buildings, or parts of buildings, that we thought might be available for purchase. Nothing usually came of those ventures, and the months dragged on as we continued meeting in the Bittsa. Then one day, Svetlana spied out two more properties and took Chuck out to take a look. The first site proved to be another dead end, but then as they drove around the city, they came to a two-story building that had the top half of it for sale. There had been a business inside, but sometime along the way the owners had decided to turn a part of it into a banya—a sauna complete with a dunking pool. The more Svetlana and Chuck looked at the building, the more they believed it could work for the church, but they weren't sure where they were because they had been driving around for such a long time. They pulled out a map and discovered they were within walking distance of the Bittsa and near the same metro stop. That was a miracle. As they exited the building, they began to believe that just maybe this was the place that God wanted them to have for our first permanent building in Russia. In all the excitement, Chuck had forgotten to ask how much it cost. When they got back to the car, he asked Svetlana about the sale price. It was $165,000—

exactly the amount of money that had been given years before to buy a church building in Russia. There are human connections, and there are God connections!

The South Korean Connection

Within a few months of arriving, we received communication from David Downs, missionary to South Korea, that he would be coming to Moscow and bringing with him one of the local pastors, Rev. Park. Little did we know that the Church of the Nazarene in South Korea was also excited about the opportunities for ministry in the former Soviet Union. David had become acquainted with Rev. Park through a project of Nazarene Missions Teams, which worked with students at Korea Nazarene University to expose them to missions. David and his wife, Susan, were missionaries for the Church of the Nazarene in Korea. The students had little to no international exposure, so various trips were organized to places across Asia.

Eventually, Rev. Park and his wife, Do-Ye, became pastors of a little church plant on the east coast of South Korea. He invited David, as his professor, to come to his church and help with the launch of an English-speaking service for those from the international community who were living nearby. Already filled with a spirit for missions, this pastor reached out to the Philippine community, as well as American GIs at the local military base. This ministry grew, and David traveled there regularly to help.

Bill Patch was the president of Korea Nazarene University, and he received a phone call from Kim Chi Chol, pastor of the Seoul Central Church. The local church wanted to sponsor a missionary to Russia, and they asked Bill who might be good for this project. At this time, it was still a bit of a challenge to have South Koreans go through the appointment system of the global Church of the Nazarene. Bill reached out to David Downs and asked him who he knew that might answer the call to move to the former Soviet Union. South Koreans have always lived in fear of Russia, and asking someone to move to Moscow would be quite terrifying. This was certainly the case when David Downs reached out to Rev. Park. Rev. Park decided that he would go up on the prayer mountain and "pray through" about this request. He spent an entire week praying and fasting, seeking the Lord's direction. At the end of that week, although it would be a real sacrifice, he and his wife, Do-Ye, said yes.

It was decided that David Downs would accompany Pastor Park on his first trip to Moscow, helping him find a place to stay and get settled in. The mission in Korea gave them $10,000 for this venture, which they took with them in cash. With the money stuffed in their socks and underwear, they flew to Moscow, arriving in the middle of the night. On the way there, they had a conversation about Rev. Park's name, Yu Sok, and whether or not that would work well in Russia. They decided to pray for the Lord to lead them, and they arrived at the biblical name of Michael, also thinking that Mr. Gorbachev had that name, so surely it would work in Russia.

When they landed, Michael Park and David Downs were a bit shaken by what they saw. Arriving at Sheremetyevo II airport in the middle of the night in the early 1990s was not for the faint of heart. The unfriendly passport control officers and the customs officials were frightening enough, but once Michael and David got out of the secure area, they were confronted with a number of shady characters who were following them around, asking them if they wanted a ride. We were in Kyiv for a few days and unable to meet them when they arrived, so we had sent a couple of people from our office to greet them. There they stood holding a little sign with the word "Nazarar," and Michael and David finally connected and were taken to the Bittsa sports complex and the place we lovingly called a hotel. It was winter, and it was very cold with lots of snow on the ground.

The next day they ventured out into the city, trying to find connections to help them get started. One major project would be finding an apartment for Michael and his family to call home. Michael was already in culture shock, for he'd never been anywhere before that he wasn't in the majority. Walking down the street, he saw a young Korean woman, and he shouted after her in Korean, only to have her turn around and try to respond with just a few words. She was the granddaughter of a North Korean, but she just spoke Russian. At that moment, he realized that he was a long way from home. However, they also had a clue that would lead them to make connections in the city. They searched out and found the North Korean Society of Russia. It was here that they found a real estate agent who helped them find an apartment within just a few days. David stayed with Michael for two weeks. We came back home to Moscow, and more connections were made. The Parks would go on to become some of our dearest friends and coworkers in the former Soviet Union.

Sometimes the connections are just what we need to get things going. Through the work and ministry of the global church, the Parks came to join us in Russia. They planted a church on the north side of Moscow but eventually transitioned their work to become a part of Global Missions. They were able to work for a time under the sponsorship of the local church, but there is nothing like the support that comes from World Evangelism Fund giving. This is the connection to the global church! Michael and Do-Ye were assigned as global missionaries for the Church of the Nazarene.

Not long after that transition, Chuck and Michael decided to take a trip to Central Asia. Being in the minority in Moscow was a bit of a challenge for the Park family, but God had something amazing in mind. The two men flew to Almaty, Kazakhstan, and began to explore the possibilities of ministry in that country. Suddenly Michael felt at home, where he and his family would no longer feel as if they were minorities in a foreign land. They weren't sure that they should begin in Almaty, so they rode the train for more than twenty-four hours to northern Kazakhstan and the city of Akmola, which literally means "white death." This was just south of Siberia and a part of the world where the Soviet Union had sent dissidents to die a slow death. Often people were sent to this part of the world on cattle cars, in the middle of winter, and dumped off with little hope of survival. The people of Akmola were originally from many nations, including Russia, Ukraine, Germany, and North Korea. Michael "prayed through" and told Chuck that the Church of the Nazarene needed to start in Akmola.

The city was a dreary place when Michael, Do-Ye, and their two children moved there. Often the city was without gas, electricity, or running water. The Parks are true heroes of the faith, who learned to work, minister, and endure through many trials. The work in Central Asia is a testament to connections, faith, and perseverance. Today there are several churches spread throughout several countries that are sharing the good news of

Jesus Christ through the Church of the Nazarene, thanks to the mysterious ways in which God speaks and mobilizes his people.

The Rest of the Story

Sometimes the pressure to succeed comes from external sources, and sometimes we simply burden ourselves with unrealistic expectations. The temptation to imagine what is "success" within the kingdom of God is always before us and rarely comes from the Lord. People will constantly want to know the results of your work, but planting seeds does not always provide visible results. Also, there are times when you encounter extremely hard soil. Trying to think strategically, we had hoped to plant a church in a place called Chekov, near the location of our youth center. It seemed reasonable in our human thinking, but nothing seemed to work. The relationships we thought we had fell through, and even today, we have no work there. However, God works in mysterious ways, and we are encouraged to participate in the Spirit's movement within the kingdom. It was about this time that we began to learn utter dependence on God. Even with a strategic plan in hand, we needed God to work and to move. At this time, we also began to embrace Matthew 19:26: "With God all things are possible." That included planting churches in the former Soviet Union.

Those hundreds of thousands of books that were handed out in the early days had made their way across the land. We would receive word of book sightings in Siberia, Central Asia, and beyond, often in kiosks where they were being sold. Just as we were discouraged about church-planting opportunities, an unexpected letter arrived at the address in Moscow printed in the books. A couple was writing to us from the town of Vyazma, about three hours west of Moscow. We had never heard of Vyazma before, but somehow one of the books had made it there. The story unfolded before us as we read the letter from Mario and Lena Russ.

Mario was originally from Cuba but had come to Saint Petersburg with the military to study. There he had met a lovely translator and language teacher, Lena. She was from Vyazma. The two fell in love and moved to Cuba to begin their new life together. It was there that they encountered family members who had found Christ. Considering that both of their home countries were Communist and atheistic, it was shocking to have relatives convert to Christianity, and yet there was something compelling about them and their lives. Eventually Mario and Lena responded to God's grace in their lives and accepted Jesus as their Savior at the Church of the Nazarene in Cuba.

Life was difficult in Cuba, and now, with two young daughters in tow, they decided to move back to Russia. Before they left, their district superintendent told them that he had heard a Russian speak at the Indianapolis General Assembly and that they ought to look for the Church of the Nazarene in Russia. The challenges in Russia were real, but Mario soon found work as a gym teacher at a high school, and Lena as a language teacher. She spoke Russian, Spanish, and English fluently and used her skills daily. However, while they were settling into their new lives in Russia, they could not find any information about the Church of the Nazarene. They prayed about how to find the church, but time was marching on.

It had been two years since Mario and Lena had arrived in Vyazma when one day they were invited to the home of the Baptist pastor. While there they noticed a book on the pastor's shelf, *The Story of Jesus the Nazarene*. The pastor picked it up and handed it to Mario, who began to leaf through it, when there at the end of the book he discovered this message: "If you want to know more about Jesus the Nazarene, write to the Church of the Nazarene in Moscow at this address." That's when he and Lena penned their letter, hoping that this was their church in Russia. Somehow, one of those little books had found its way to the right place at the right time.

Jay and Teanna Sunberg had come and joined the team by then. They headed out to Vyazma, where they met Mario and Lena and the whole family. God had a strategic plan in mind. Eventually, two Nazarene churches were planted in Vyazma. Mario became the pastor of one of them. They went on to have a son, Danil, who was born in Russia. Their youngest daughter studied for the ministry and married a Nazarene pastor from Ukraine, and they became pioneer church planters in Moldova. Sadly, Lena died far too early in life, while receiving treatment for leukemia. She had been the district secretary for the Moscow North District, and I'm happy to say, as such, signed my ordination certificate. Just when our personal strategic plan didn't pan out, God revealed to us a much bigger plan. God had already been at work, tying together the strings that were borne out of a faithful walk with Christ, even in what appeared to be the ordinary and mundane. Handing out books at a subway station. Hearing someone speak at general assembly. Watching the transformed life of a relative. Writing a letter. Somehow, we began to really understand, "with God all things are possible."

The story of Larissa in the introduction is real. She was our next-door neighbor when we lived on Ulitsa Maria Ulyanova. She and her husband, Timofei, became dear friends, and it was through another circumstance of prevenient grace that Timofei began attending church with us. A coworker from Volgograd, Nina, had locked herself out of our apartment and rang Timofei's doorbell. There, over a cup of tea, she told him about the missionaries who had moved in next door and the church they had started. Little did she know that at that moment, he found himself dejected, because everything in which he had placed his hope had come crashing down around him. He had served the Communist Party well and had given his mind to develop a computer system that still flew in MiG jets today, but it seemed that everything he had believed in no longer existed. He was a man in search of truth.

After Larissa and Timofei had attended church for nearly a year, I found myself locked out of the apartment one day and rang the bell to Timofei and Larissa's apartment. She wasn't home, but Timofei ushered me in and put on the teapot. There in their small living room, he began to talk to me about his life. He showed me a red ID card and holder; he told me that it was his membership in the devil's party—the Communist Party. As we sat there that day, I asked him about his walk with Jesus and told him that although he had come to church for a year, I'd not seen him give his life to Christ. He told me that Jesus couldn't forgive him. At that time, I had no idea what he had done, nor what his role had been in the Communist Party. All I knew was that Jesus had died to forgive our sins and that gift was for everyone. With his Communist ID card on the table, he prayed with me to ask Jesus to forgive him of his sins, and in that moment, Timofei was born again.

It's always a joy to watch a new believer grow and develop in his or her faith, and Timofei was no different. He would often come to our apartment with a new question or to get another book to read. He studied voraciously everything that we could give him. During the summer months, he and Larissa would go out to the dacha to escape the city and grow vegetables to help them survive the winter. They were so worried that we didn't have a garden somewhere, and they always made sure to share their vegetables with us. It became an annual ritual to make chocolate zucchini cake in September, when they would bring me the most delicious zucchini. They seemed amused by what I would cook up, but they enjoyed it too.

After Timofei gave his life to Christ, he would tell people, "I was Saul, but now I'm Paul." Every day he grew in his faith. One September, he asked me if I could drive him out to his dacha to pick up Larissa, their bird and cat, and their vegetables. They didn't have a car, and we had one with a hatchback that could haul a large load, so I agreed. I wasn't always excited about driving because it could be a real challenge. Our car was a challenge, a Lada Niva 4X4 that improved our prayer lives because we had to pray daily that it wouldn't break down. The police were always a challenge because they liked to pull you over and question you—just because. Finally, I had failed to anticipate the challenge of having someone who had never driven give directions. But before we pulled out of the driveway, Timofei asked me if he could pray for our trip to the dachas that day. He pulled a piece of paper out of his breast pocket and unfolded it to reveal a prayer he had written and prepared for the journey. It was beautiful as he prayed for God to be with us, lead us, and protect us. I was amazed at his spiritual growth.

The trip to the dacha was rather uneventful, except for the few times I had to quickly change lanes because Timofei hadn't given me enough warning that we were turning! We had driven for about an hour and a half and were now out on a country road when he pointed to his dacha, just ahead and on the right. What he failed to mention to me was that there was a ditch on the side of the road that was crossable on a small concrete bridge that led to his dacha. None of this was visible because of the tall grass and weeds. I turned to the right to reach the dacha, thinking it was a solid path, but overshot the little bridge and ended up teetering over the edge, with the front of the car in the ditch and with the back wheels up in the air. This was not good! We climbed out of the car, and Timofei walked to the dacha to get Larissa while I examined the situation. It looked as if all I needed was someone to pull me out of the ditch. The car didn't look damaged. Walking to the road, I flagged down a car, which had a tow rope (you always needed one), and they pulled me out of the ditch in a jiffy. I straightened out the car and pulled up to the dacha, where Timofei and Larissa were already bringing out all the goods to load into the car. In went the vegetables, zucchini, tomatoes, potatoes, cabbages, turnips, beets, cucumbers, and more. Next came the cat, and finally, Larissa and the bird piled into the back seat. In a short time, we were ready to head back to the city.

We had driven a couple of kilometers down the road when suddenly I heard a terrible noise from under the car. When I looked into my rearview mirror, I could see car parts strewn across the road. It looked as though the drive shaft had fallen off. Pulling over, we collected everything we could find and put the parts in the back seat with Larissa. Surely another vehicle could tow us to the next village, where someone could repair the car. The next driver who stopped informed us that it would be hopeless to go to the next village. Although that village once had two repair shops, the competition between the proprietors had become so heated that they had recently shot and killed each other, and now there was no one left to fix a car. Timofei and I talked, but he was unfamiliar with cars and had no idea what to do, so I suggested we try to return to the dacha, where at least we would be safe for the night. A large crane was coming toward us on the road, so we stepped in front of it until it stopped. The crane operator hitched us on to the back and towed us to the dacha.

By this time the police had set up a roadblock across the street and were collecting frustrated drivers as they confiscated their vehicles. I gingerly made my way across the street, praying that, just maybe, these would be nice policemen who might be able to provide some assistance. That was a wrong assumption. They didn't want to help, nor did they want me to talk to them. However, a stranded driver heard me and asked if he could be of some assistance. Why not? The car was a four-wheel-drive model, and as he examined the damage, he said he thought he could rig the vehicle to operate as a two-wheel drive to get us home. All he needed was a wire coat hanger! One was found, and to this day, I'm not sure what he did to the car, but he assured us it would work.

At this point, I was a little nervous about driving the car, so I asked him where he was going. The police had taken his car, and he needed to get back to Moscow. I asked him if he would be willing to drive my damaged vehicle to Moscow with the rest of us as passengers, and he agreed. So this stranger got in the driver's seat, and I joined Larissa in the back seat with the cat, bird, and the drive shaft, and we made our way back to the city. The car worked reasonably well, and we made it to one of the police checkpoints on the ring around Moscow. Our stranger told us that this was where he needed to get out, so I jumped into the driver's seat and drove us the rest of the way home. As we pulled onto Ulitsa Maria Ulyanova, my heart was filled with relief to finally see our apartment building. I was also a bit tense from the entire journey, but at that moment Timofei said, "Isn't it amazing the way God answered my prayer!" To be honest, I had forgotten about the prayer, but Timofei had not. He looked at me and asked, "Do you think that was an angel who drove the car home?" The former secretary of the Moscow Communist Party was teaching me a lesson in faith.

Merriam-Webster's Collegiate Dictionary tells us that a pioneer is "a person or group that originates or helps open up a new line of thought or activity or a new method or technical development" or "one of the first to settle in a territory."[1] It's all about doing something new and creating pathways where none have existed in the past. As a follower of Jesus Christ, we discover that he goes ahead of us and prepares the way for us, if only we will follow him. We learn that we are not really pioneers, but the Lord is the pioneer, and as we abide in him, we will recognize his paths. When societal shifts begin to happen, when walls come crashing down and new opportunities are placed before us, we must not be paralyzed by fear. Instead, we embrace the reality of the presence of Jesus and his words that "with God all things are possible."

1. *Merriam-Webster's Collegiate Dictionary*, s.v. "pioneer," accessed January 17, 2025, https://unabridged.merriam-webster.com/collegiate/pioneer.

Epilogue

THERE WILL ALWAYS BE new opportunities for ministry in this world. The geopolitical shifts may not be as seismic as they were in those few years when the Iron Curtain came down, but they do continue to occur. While we have excellent schools, universities, and seminaries around the world, far too often, we do not examine what it may take to pioneer a new work. Maybe it's because we feel that the pioneer days are over and that we need to focus on building on the foundations that we have already laid. However, with migration and population shifts, new opportunities for pioneer work are appearing nearly every day.

We wish to encourage a new generation of pioneers to embrace the call of God to go and make Christlike disciples in the nations, cities, towns, and neighborhoods where there may be little or no Christian presence. Will it look like it did when the Iron Curtain came down? Probably not, but to be a pioneer is to step out into varied spaces, try new things, be willing to make mistakes, and show the love of Jesus to this world. Just maybe God has an "Item 15" in store for you!

Afterword

THIS INSPIRING RECOUNTING of the beginning of the Church of the Nazarene in the former Soviet Union is dedicated to "all the people who are not mentioned in these pages." Christianity's most well-known pioneering missionary wrote with a similar affection for those who had been "[partners] in the gospel from the first day until now" (Phil. 1:5).

From the inception of Nazarene missions, there has been a partnership between those who have gone as missionaries and those who have supported them in prayer and generous giving. For one hundred years, Nazarenes have given to the World Evangelism Fund (previously General Budget) through Faith Promise and Easter and Thanks offerings.

The World Evangelism Fund (WEF) is the cornerstone of Nazarene missions giving. It is the primary means of financial support for our globally commissioned missionaries, including salaries and health care. Likewise, WEF provides the means for infrastructure support for all our missionaries and coordination of our mission initiatives.

Because of this partnership, the Church of the Nazarene is now in 165 countries and world areas. However, millions of people still have never heard the good news or experienced the life-changing power of Jesus. Thus there is still a great need for those who will respond, "Here am I. Send me!" (Isa. 6:8). Along with these, there is the need for partners who will pray sincerely and give generously. Together in the Spirit, we can make real and eternal differences.

Our Lord has commissioned us to "go and make disciples of all nations" (Matt. 28:19). As we pray and go and give, we can anticipate that God again will "do exceedingly abundantly above all that we ask or think" (Eph. 3:20, NKJV).

—Geoff Kunselman
Stewardship Development Director
International Church of the Nazarene

A Word from Nazarene Missions International

God is always at work drawing people to himself. He works through many denominations, organizations, and individuals, and we celebrate every time a person is redeemed.

The story told in *Pulling Back the Curtain on the Former Soviet Union*, though, is ours to celebrate in a unique way. During a pivotal time in world history, God worked powerfully through the Church of the Nazarene to bring hope and healing to the former Soviet Union. As you read this engaging book by Franklin Cook and Carla Sunberg, I hope you feel proud of your Nazarene brothers and sisters who stepped bravely through newly opened doors to share the gospel. And as the authors remind us, notice that the "going" was made possible by a vast army of Nazarenes who prayed earnestly and gave sacrificially. Many of you were part of that army. Thank you for the role you played.

I pray this gripping story from the past will inspire you to engage fully with the missionary work of the present. For many places in the world, TODAY is the pivotal moment for God's transformational work. Let's pray and give and go so that God can continue to write beautiful stories of redemption through us!

—Cheryl Crouch
Global Nazarene Missions International Director

To hear more from Cheryl and her personal experience in the former Soviet Union, scan the following QR code.